Passionate

by Elizabeth Parker

Passionate

This book is dedicated to all of my readers out there. I appreciate you and your support! It's also dedicated to those who have made it a point to live their lives with a passion. You're an inspiration. To the writers or soon-to-be writers, good luck to you in your future endeavors!

First Edition
ISBN-13: 978-1530373659
ISBN-10: 1530373654

A portion of the proceeds from the sales of this book will be donated to an animal rescue group.

Lesson 18-Enjoy Life! _____ 243

Just noticing the simplicity of my dogs' happiness is enough to make me realize that it is often the little things in life that are most important. _____ 248 Nothing brightens up the day like a big smile from your pups upon entering the room! _____ 248 Being a hero to someone, even if it is a dog, is a feeling like no other. Though it can be frustrating, it can be the most rewarding thing to give someone a second chance at a happy life. _____ 250

The only thing wrong with trying to please everyone is that there's always, at least, one person who will remain unhappy. You. _ 251 Remember, just because someone is smiling, it doesn't mean they aren't holding back tears.___ 252 What makes someone better than someone else? The answer? Nothing. Everyone has their own weaknesses._____ 254 Often, the reason that you make mistakes is to learn from them and teach someone else. ___ 255

Prologue-Learn from Your Dogs, No Manual Required

It's been a long time since I've done this. Over six years to be exact. The last time I had written about lessons learned from a rescue dog began with Buddy Senior in my first published book, Finally Home: Lessons on Life from a Free-Spirited Dog.

It is a book that explores the journey that many dog lovers have experienced, rescuing a dog that was not quite a puppy, but acted more like an unruly fur ball that could melt the most hardened of hearts. I've learned a lot since then which helped govern the way in which I live.

Of course, with writing and putting one's heartfelt, most innermost thoughts out there for the world to see, some had understood the trials and tribulations, and some didn't quite get the possibility of such a dog.

Buddy Sr. was a handful, especially for a twenty-something-year-old couple who didn't quite have the knowledge of how to undo certain behaviors that accompanied such a dog. The book outlined the mistakes we had made, the lessons we had learned from not only understanding such a dog but understanding life through the eyes of a dog.

Those lessons built a strong foundation of things to come, of dogs rescued, of future teachings that we would need to learn, and how to love unconditionally with patience, understanding, and heck, just learning how to enjoy life.

Since Buddy Senior, my home has been open to several rescue dogs, some that we fostered, others that have become an integral part of my family. They had either suffered neglect, been unloved, or were viewed as unadoptable in the eyes of some, yet each had individual qualities that taught valuable lessons.

And those lessons all apply to life as we live it, goals that we want to achieve and writing. Be passionate!

Lesson 1-Look Deeper, but See This Time

Back in the year 2000, Buddy Senior came into our lives—a firecracker full of spark—determined to make us transform him into a respectable pup. Ten years later, after years of his antics, I sat on the couch with him by my side and penned a book that I knew he would appreciate. It was, after all, a book all about him.

The book chronicled his life as I knew it, and my life as I would come to know it, as it soon followed an entirely different path.

After he passed away from Osteosarcoma the same year Finally Home was published, I then penned a different kind of book. The book, called Final Journey, described what it was truly like to lose a dog and how the grieving process affected our family. It was the first of its kind (that I know of). What I hadn't fully written about after that was Buddy Junior's life, the precious dog we had adopted after Buddy Senior's death.

I had introduced him in Final Journey, but never really told his story. Not in detail anyway.

It was mere coincidence that Buddy Senior and Junior shared the same name. To distinguish between the two in conversation, we called Buddy Senior "Buddy Thomas" and Buddy Junior "Buddy Joe." (Doesn't everyone give their dogs middle names)?

Buddy Joe was a plush white golden retriever, with light brown eyes that I swear showed the brilliance and innocence of his precious soul. He had the sweetest disposition and captured our hearts immediately.

He was very shy and extremely gentle. When he first came to our house, we were told by the rescue group that he wouldn't eat for the first few days. Well, as many dog lovers will attest, bacon can usually lure the shyest of dogs out of a corner, so the first action we took was to cook some and let the intoxicating aroma permeate the air.

While our other two dogs—Brandi and Toffee—drooled with delight, Buddy Joe lifted his head from his safety spot in the corner and sniffed around. Within minutes, his large body got up and slowly walked toward the delicious smell.

First crisis averted. He ate.

As with many rescue dogs, it took a little while for him to come out of his shell. Not knowing much about his previous life, all we could do was let him take his time and join the pack as he felt comfortable. Day by day, he became more at home, and his sisters welcomed him with open paws.

He was a funny dog. Although he was afraid of his own shadow, he had graceful tendencies that made everyone smile.

When he came to us, he didn't even know his name. We had to teach him. He feared anything that "clicked" or made noise. The television startled him, as did boxes or any abrupt loud noise. Let's not even mention the vacuum cleaner, as this was his sworn enemy. Sadly, cameras terrified him the most. The moment a camera was in his presence, he'd bolt into another room or try to hide in a corner, under the bed—anywhere he couldn't be noticed. As such, we didn't have many pictures of him due to his fear. Only afterward when it was too late, did we discover what caused that fear.

Once he became more comfortable, he demonstrated special heartwarming qualities that made me love him dearly. For instance, when we would get ready to go for a walk, I'd leash one of the girls first and then him. I can only imagine that he'd thought I had forgotten to leash him, as he would stand faithfully by his leash as if to say, "Mom! You have to leash me! I can't possibly go on a walk by myself!" And he was right. Buddy Joe was a runner, and although he was happy, I was never quite sure how far he could run. One thing was for certain...he was lightning fast!

Only when he was at the doggy park or a fenced enclosure would I let him run, and run he would! Like many dogs, he enjoyed barking at the birds that congregated in the bushes. Though he had never caught one, you could always determine where he was by the flock of birds that encompassed the sky in a quick scurry.

The most cherished part of his walk, however, was when we approached a specific house. The owners of this house had a dog that would hear us coming and then dart toward the gate, back and forth, making quite a racket. Buddy Joe would pull us on his leash each and every time he heard this dog. He would then watch with wonder, for as long as we let him, at this fanatical dog with an exorbitant amount of energy. I suppose he was trying to understand what would make this dog act so crazy. Of course, we didn't stay long as not to upset the sassy dog (or his owners). However, Buddy would have stayed there for hours if he had his say!

In addition to birds and his obsession with the dog by the gate, he was fascinated by other animals. In Las Vegas, especially during the colder months, the ground is very hard. One night after letting him outside in the backyard, I heard the gate frantically banging back and forth. Brandi and Toffee showed no interest, however, Buddy Joe went to investigate and much to his pleasant surprise, found a bunny trying to escape. The moment I saw it, my heart dropped. It was too late. Buddy Joe was ready for his second dinner. He did catch the rabbit but luckily dropped it at my command. The frightened bunny ran toward Brandi and Toffee, who watched the rabbit run under their legs, unfazed by the entire scene. I'm thrilled to report the bunny made it out of the yard unscathed, and Buddy Joe couldn't be prouder that he actually "caught" a rabbit, if only for a brief moment.

There were traits about Buddy Joe that were incredibly delightful. For one, he adored his tiny stuffed animals and loved pawing at them first before grabbing them in his mouth. He was never shy about what he wanted, such as punching the door with his big paw to go outside. And he had the most amazing howl. "A-wooooooooo!!" This howl was usually during a stretch or in an attempt to say good morning to us.

Buddy manned his spot by the glass sliding door in the kitchen like a faithful guard. From his spot, he loved to stand and greet passer-bys with his radiant smile, wagging tail, and deep bark.

Similar to peek-a-boo with children, Buddy Joe showed amusement when one would hide behind an object and then pop out from nowhere. His tail whipped with enthusiasm each and every time, causing an onset of giggles from whoever initiated the game.

He was the only boy dog we had that loved to kiss. As he sat on the couch, if someone sat in front of him, they could expect an endless amount of slobber to land on their cheek and then he would hide his face as if embarrassed, only to start kissing a few moments later. Most loved his attention, except for Brandi—our alpha, who would warn him with a low growl. That didn't stop him, however. I guess he figured he'd win her heart over eventually!

Two years to the day after we adopted him, I have the fondest memory of taking him for a long walk, just him and I, to celebrate his "gotcha day." It was such a radiant morning; the sun was shining, but it wasn't too hot, and he was so excited to go on his walk.

As the day progressed, I had cooked all of the dogs an egg— sunny side up—and some bacon. Of course, they devoured it with splendor.

It wasn't until that night when I was getting them ready to retire for the evening that I rubbed his throat and felt something that hadn't been there before. Two large bumps about the same size, on both sides. As if by instinct, I knew. I dropped to the floor and hugged him, praying I was wrong.

Breaking the cardinal rule about researching illnesses on the Internet, I searched for what those bumps could indicate, and all sites pointed to the same conclusion. Lymphoma.

How I hoped those sites were wrong. How I tried to talk myself out of it as I frantically left a message at the veterinarian's office for a first appointment Monday morning. How I wished the day would have ended on a better note.

But, fate had already been determined.

After our visit to the veterinarian, I had learned that Buddy Joe did, indeed have lymphoma. This beautiful, sweet, innocent baby was only ten years old, but a deadly form of cancer had lodged its way into his body.

I had my doubts about chemotherapy since it didn't work with Buddy Senior, but after learning that the odds were better with lymphoma, decided to give it a try.

It was only two weeks before he an adverse reaction to the therapy and became very ill with a fever and lethargy. After visiting the emergency hospital and our regular vet, there was nothing they could do. Buddy Joe's short life and short time with us were over, but the impact he made on our lives was enormous.

The most difficult part of losing him was finding out just WHY he was so afraid of cameras, cell phones, anything that clicked or made loud noises or shined bright lights.

While he was in the emergency hospital, an X-ray of his lungs was taken to see if there was any obstruction. The X-ray showed that a BB was lodged very close to his lungs. Now, it had been there for years and wasn't affecting his breathing as he was shot BEFORE we ever adopted him. However, someone apparently shot this poor pup with a BB gun, scaring the courage out of him and leaving a BB in his body as a reminder until the day he died. My heart had broken in pieces upon seeing this evidence on the X-ray. I don't know how anyone could be violent toward any animal, but especially don't understand how they could have shot this one. He was too precious for words.

We lost him to cancer on October 24th, 2012.

So what was the lesson you may ask?

Very Simple. **Look deeper, but see this time.**

For the two short years that we had Buddy Joe, we couldn't comprehend his fear of cameras. It's just a click and a flash.

But, just because we didn't know what had happened in this poor dog's past, doesn't mean that something didn't exist. We knew there had to have been a reason he was afraid, but couldn't determine the cause.

The same rule applies to people. As we venture on this journey of life, we meet dozens, hundreds, thousands along the way.

Some are completely transparent, without an air of mystery to them.

Others, well, not so much. They look perfectly healthy and even happy on the outside, but they are guarded, or secretive. They seem solid on the surface, but there is something about them they aren't revealing.

Perhaps it is because they are simply private. There is a chance, however, that their wounds run deep, and keeping themselves guarded is the only way to protect themselves. They don't necessarily have to disclose all, at least not until they are ready. Sometimes you need to look closely and realize; there's more than meets the surface.

Which brings me to the next lesson learned.

Lesson 2-A Little Kindness Goes a Long Way

It's easy to be kind to any dog I meet, or any animal for that matter. I have utmost respect and admiration for them and find innocence in even the most ferocious. They do what comes naturally or what they need to do to survive.

Kindness is key and dogs know this. Buddy Joe knew this with every stranger he approached. He was shyer than most, yet went out on a limb to "smile" upon meeting someone. Dogs don't think of the consequences if they cozy up to a stranger and wag their tail—a dog's way of indicating friendliness. It's just something that is instinctive.

With people, it's not always so easy to apply those same principles.

Let's face it. Some people have a chip on their shoulder from the moment you meet them. They are ready to chomp at the bit or argue continuously about any given topic at any given time. It's difficult if not impossible to get through to them, no matter how hard you try and no matter which angle you take. Aside from agreeing with their every word, (which even then can cause an unforeseen controversy), this person just won't find their merry place in your presence, or anyone else's for that matter. All in all, they are not the most charismatic of people.

Those people do exist. And I'll be the first to confess that I don't have much patience in dealing with them.

But there are others. A cashier at the local store, or a flight attendant, or a stranger in the street might appear to be having a bad day. But, for all you know, he or she could be enduring a bad couple of days, weeks, or even months!

You might just meet them on a day where they are a little snippy or agitated and don't feel as much positive energy as you do at that precise moment.

These are the people who might desperately need a congenial smile, or words of encouragement, or a good-natured joke to soften the mood. You never know what has happened to them. Though they seem like everyone else, they might have just lost their son or daughter, or just suffered another type of major loss in life, or discovered they have a fatal illness. We just never know.

I'll admit; it's a gamble. If they are the type of a person who is motivated to be despondent, well, then you might have just wasted your breath, but nothing more.

However, sometimes giving a person a compliment, or finding a way to make them smile might be very effective and just what they need.

As an example, have you ever thought the world was against you, even for just one day in your life? Perhaps the dry cleaner attendant lost your favorite suit, right after you got into a fender bender in the parking lot, but right before you discovered that you were losing your job? We all have good and bad days, but sometimes the bad days can be overpowering and seem like dark clouds are following us everywhere.

Hearing a word of kindness from a stranger can help a person realize that, hey, maybe the *entire* world isn't evil. Perhaps there *is* that one person who is quite gracious.

Does it take a lot of effort to smile at a stranger or do something nice for someone, such as holding open a door? A little token of kindness can make a difference in someone's day.

Now, what you read next might seem like a contradiction. However, I assure you, it's not!

Lesson 3-Use Your Judgment

I've had dogs all of my life, but for the past sixteen years or so, all I've had are golden retrievers and duck tollers—two breeds that are affable to anyone for the most part, so I have to say that their judgment might be somewhat questionable! But in all honesty, not really. As friendly as they are, their judgment is usually right on target.

Dogs are intelligent souls, but they only have their senses to guide them when determining who to trust and who is a "bad seed."

Although dogs cannot converse in the same language that we do, I trust their instinct wholeheartedly. Now, while I haven't owned a vicious dog, I will watch my dogs' reactions upon meeting people for the first time. And, I have noticed that the moment one of my dogs cower in the corner, or aren't as sociable as they usually are, I get a disquieting chill down my spine. In fact, I can't help but watch this newly introduced person intently to discern what my dog is detecting.

I would venture a bet that the same type of chill comes over my dogs, except they are unable to articulate. They can't possibly explain it to me in a way that I'd understand. They don't have to reason, they just have their senses.

Needless to say, my dogs have never been wrong. Not ever. It doesn't necessarily mean that the unwelcomed person was evil or a serial killer, but just that there was something alarming about them. Each and every time, it was proven. Perhaps the person lacked integrity. Or perhaps they weren't of the highest character or didn't like dogs. But it was something.

I believe that people have that same instinct, but since we might not know exactly why we feel the way we do about meeting this new person, we choose to disregard our instinct, and wind up regretting it later!

Have you ever met someone who, for some reason, although you couldn't quite put your finger on it, you didn't like? There was probably nothing tangible about this meeting that you could explain while still appearing sane in the process. However, you got a funny feeling when this person approached.

This type of situation had happened more times than not in my life, and sadly, there had been times when I have completely ignored my instinct and tried to let logic prevail.

The only problem with relying on logic is that most of the time our inner feelings are correct. After getting burned way too many times, I have decided to listen more to my gut instinct than to logic...especially if I get a strong negative vibe upon meeting someone.

If only we weren't programmed to apply reasoning to why we feel the way that we do, we could probably weed the harmful people out of our life before they even had a chance to walk in. Use your judgment and trust your instincts!

Lesson 4-Have a Plan

Can you do this?

Elizabeth Parker

Is your dog on a schedule? Do they eat breakfast at the same time every morning, wait for you by the door when you come home from work, and eat dinner at the same time each night?

I always have my dogs on a schedule. While it's sometimes difficult to adhere to that schedule—especially if I want to sleep late or stop at the store after work— I do my best to be there exactly when my dogs are expecting me.

Now, on days when I'm home, I am under the strong impression that my dogs have formulated a plan.

They are accustomed to dining at 5:00 PM.   Around 4:00 PM, however, they begin to get antsy. That is when one of them, who was most likely richly appointed by the other, will start becoming a slight bit unruly. This, in turn, prompts the other one to get up and about. They then collaborate until I begin to pay attention.

It starts at a quiet pace, then escalates by them throwing their toys in the air, until they finally lose patience (now around 4:30 PM), and begin with the nudging. If you have dogs, this may sound familiar to you.

The bulk of my work is done on a computer, so it's at around this time that one (or both) of my dogs will begin nudging the laptop in an effort to knock it off of my lap.

When that doesn't work, the dogs extend their paws and start giving high fives. Usually, one looks for reciprocation while the other paces, pants, grabs their toys and circles the room to break my concentration and focus on them.

Then there's me, trying diligently to stick to their regularly programmed schedule and not surrender, but depending on how badly they want their meal, their plan is to distract me so much, that I oblige and feed them early.

I hang my head in shame and acknowledge that sometimes, their plan works. Hey, I'm only human.

Do dogs sit up at night and write magnificent notes describing exactly how they want to implement this plan? Do they contemplate how to get more cookies during the day? Well, no, although sometimes I tend to think so. They do, however, team up to con me into doing what they want. Bullies!

Of course in the human world, we work a little differently. We have the ability to outline and organize what our goals are in life, sketch them out and work towards them. Sometimes, twists and unforeseen circumstances emerge and get in the way. However, it's always good to be prepared, and yes, have a plan!

For many of us, part of that plan involves personal and professional relationships and employment. Unless you live and work your dream job, work isn't always a walk in the park. (That is unless you're a dog walker and if so, kudos to you)!

This chapter is considerably longer than most, as it's important in one's professional life to have a plan and not be caught in a vulnerable position.

Whether you are a calm, cool and collected individual or one who flies off the handle at the drop of a dime, each of us has our personalized boiling point, causing the whistle on our tea kettle of life to scream. We each have a limited threshold for which no one should ever cross. It may take one event, or it may take fifty, but once that foot crosses the line, we make the decision to cut all ties.

As we build relationships throughout our life, we begin by acting on our best behavior. We often conform just enough to appease the other party, whether it is a friend, boyfriend, girlfriend or boss. Then, as the relationship grows, we may also find that we have slipped off those rose colored glasses and begin to see the person for who they are.

If we are lucky, that person will continue to dazzle us as we get to know them. Those are the people with whom you want to formulate relationships. Those are the ones who are straight shooters and honest—good, bad or indifferent. They have integrity, honor, respect and they also have your back in a heartbeat, no questions asked. They legitimately care about you, and it shows.

Often, however, we are faced with the opposite. Those are the ones who are either selfish or narcissistic. Initially, they may fool us into believing they are a good person to know, but in time, we find out differently. Their act was fundamentally stellar. Their actions, however, were inconsistent. Eventually, that person reveals that it is predominately all about them. All-the-time.

It can be difficult to weed these people out of our circle. They appear genuine, responsive and industrious, in a pragmatic attempt to make us one of their followers. That is until we discover that they aren't listening to what *we* have to say, or even if we begin the conversation, it always ends by discussing their wants, needs, and desires, throwing our initial ideas by the wayside.

When it is a friend or intimate relationship, you can choose to walk out.

In an employer/employee relationship, we often need to keep our jobs to make that green stuff we call money. It's not so easy to stroll out the door.

There are so many situations in the workplace that can contribute to our unhappiness. The reasons?

There are too many to list. Some employers find it acceptable to give twenty-five percent more work in addition to a pay-cut. They may think it is okay not to pay you on time, or ask you to work holidays after they gave you the day off. There are even some who find nothing wrong with ridiculing you in front of your peers or making demands that are simply not possible. The fault is always with you and not because of something they've done. The range of causes that lead to unhappiness can vary greatly.

It is these types of relationships that become more difficult to leave. They have you right where they want you.

Unfortunately, most of us need to work and sometimes it is not doing the things we love. Even if the salary might not be top-notch, perhaps we depend on them to pay for our family's benefits. Often, we feel stuck.

Because of this reason, I always find it necessary to have another job in your back pocket...or, at least, a potential job. I believe it is wise to go on interviews, even if you have no intention of leaving your current employer. Every interview is like a dress-rehearsal. In an indirect way, it is a skill. It helps to build self-confidence as well.

Think about this. If you work at a company long enough, it may be ten years (or more) before you have to go on an actual interview. Since an interview is the type of meeting you don't encounter frequently, the uncertainty causes many to develop high anxiety and fear attending the actual interview. If you schedule interviews frequently, however, you become more comfortable, especially if you go to one when you do not need a job. Plus, you never know if there is something else out there for you! Sadly, when you need a job, you become more desperate, and the anxiety increases.

Unfortunately, when some employers know that you have no other alternatives, they figure that they call the shots. I won't say this for all because there are some employers with hearts of gold.

There are also some who have hearts of steel, however, and once they realize that the ball is always in their court, that is when they know they can take full advantage...and often do. They only think about business first, forgetting that their loyal employees are real people with families.

One thing I learned is that if possible, never leave a job until you have another one lined up and try to have at least six months of living expenses saved just in case your new job isn't quite the dream you had planned.

While it is wonderful to have a job that you love, I find dependency is a very tough and vulnerable situation. It is important to at least try to be prepared for anything. Though we cannot predict the future or know what obstacles are going to drift our way, we can take calculated steps to do everything we can in preparation for that rainy day.

These principles helped me a great deal in 2001, right after September 11th. I was working for an air-freight company, and as we all listened intently to the horrific news, the owner walked around saying "This is not going to be good for business." Never mind the horror that was taking place only miles away, but his focus was on his business, not the people.

Needless to say, the day after, I was let go from my job, as were all new employees. While I had experience in the technical support field, support jobs—which had originally taken up eight pages of the classified pages—decreased to half of one page. It was clear that I had to make a choice and quickly learn a new trade if I was ever going to become gainfully employed again.

As I searched through those few ads, I noticed that Visual Basic jobs were plentiful compared to most. That very day, I bought a "Teach Yourself Visual Basic" book and spent the next two months learning it, all day, every day. By the end of two months, I had taught myself a great deal.

Luckily I did find a job with a former employer and was able to utilize my new-found skills. Since then, I realized how important it was to gain knowledge of new areas of expertise and keep yourself informed. Keep learning and pick up vital skills.

Broaden your knowledge base!

Becoming and remaining resourceful can help you maneuver through the toughest of times. While it requires you to step outside of the realm for which you feel comfortable, it's helpful, just in case jobs in that field become scarce. You never know what can trigger high unemployment, so it's beneficial to become mindfully prepared. There's nothing worse than being blindsided and not having anywhere to go or inadequate skills to become competitive in the already flooded job market.

During a troubled economy, there are many people seeking

employment opportunities and those who already have a job are repeatedly told, "You're just lucky to have a job!"

While that may be true and deserved of merit, every job has its good and bad points. For the most part, you just have to hope that the good outweighs the bad.

What appears 'good' to one employee, may not matter much to another.

Each person is motivated differently. For some, money may be the driving factor. Makes sense, right? After all, we all work or want to work to collect a salary. But what are the trade-offs and at what cost?

What if you are offered a fantastic salary? However, there are no benefits, no 401k, no vacation days. Or better yet, long grueling hours without any time to yourself or with family.

Or, vice versa. Fabulous benefits, three weeks paid time off —but the salary leaves much to be desired. How about flexibility? Does your lifestyle require you to have some wiggle room in your work schedule? Do you need access to a full-time daycare center? How about a job that enables you to take your pet to work? Does it matter how the boss treats the employees as long as they compensate well? What about how the boss treats the clients (or patients, or animals- whichever the case may be). Is it important for you to have an honest relationship with your boss that allows you to give criticism safely, as well as receive it without any negative repercussions? Do you require constant praise? Supervision? The ability to work independently? Work as a team? Is structure important? Or do you thrive on taking calculated risks?

I know—there are a lot of questions.

When you go to a job interview, do you already know how much you'll be willing to give in return for a job?

I don't know if there's such a thing as 'the perfect career' however since most of us spend forty hours or more there, it should be somewhat intriguing. I usually make an itemized list before I even go on an interview determining what my desirable 'guidelines' for my next career path.

We all know that the first ninety days is considered a probation period, but would you agree that a new boss is ALSO on probation in our eyes? Isn't it a two-way street? Shouldn't the new boss also be on their best behavior?

What's important to you as an individual? What motivates you to work harder and be successful? What's your perfect dream job and does it exist?

Either way, it's a good idea always to have a plan just in case that rainy day does come. If the dream job doesn't exist, of course, we need to work. But it's helpful to have a plan and in your free time, explore your hobbies with a passion!

Job Hunting Tips

In the past when jobs were plentiful, it was almost a surefire guarantee that if you have an updated resume, you were well groomed, had a pleasant personality and the necessary qualifications, you would get the job that you sought after.

Unfortunately, with so much competition pounding the pavement, it's time for job candidates to raise the bar on their potential employer's expectations, think out of the box and rise above the rest when beginning the job search.

Whether you are staying in the realm of your current career path or deciding to switch, research will be a key element in putting you on the correct course. Research everything you can about the position, the qualifications, the company and even the current employees. You want to make sure that not only are you a good fit for the position but that the position is a good fit for you, as well.

❖ Spend each day as if job hunting was your actual job. Don't randomly apply to jobs. Instead, look for the ones that closely resemble where you would like to work.

❖ Network. These days there are many social media networking tools. Tell everyone you know that you are looking for a job. Join popular social media sites. Talk to people. Someone you know might know of a company that is hiring.

- ❖ Look at Internet Job Listings.
- ❖ Don't forget to look in the newspapers!
- ❖ Attend job fairs. You might not find your dream job there. But, you might. Every opportunity is worth a shot.
- ❖ Do you have a good rapport with previous employers? Why not give them a call and see if there are any openings?
- ❖ Know the company for which you are applying. Since you are going through the trouble of

finding the perfect fit, you don't want to work for a company that is not a good match. Make sure the distance falls within your desired commute time. If you require benefits, make sure that this company is offering, at least, part of the compensation package that you require. There's nothing wrong with going for an interview to learn about the company. Also, try not to look at interviews as a waste of time if you don't get the job. They truly are helpful and are learning experiences for your next interview. Think of "failed" interviews as warm-ups which will provide you with a variety of common questions asked and allow you to hone your interview skills to achieve the job you seek.

❖ Be certain that you can do the job. It's not a good idea to apply just for the sake of applying if you can't follow through. It will be frustrating for you to accept a job offer if you don't truly have the qualifications, as well as frustration for the team that trains you. Be sure your qualifications and skills match the job for which you are applying.

❖ Make sure your resume is clean. It should be in a nice,

neat format that is easily legible. Ensure that your timeline of previous employment is understandable and accurate. If there are any time lapses, be prepared to explain them. Also, one of the most important things is to make sure there are no spelling or grammatical errors. Make sure that it is updated, including your most current phone number and email address. Try to have an email address that is not xxx@xxx.com. It should be something respectable. Also, make sure your cover letter is precise and to the point, again making you stand out from the crowd. Try to avoid cookie-cutter cover letters and resumes.

❖ If you are going to give references, confer with at least three prior bosses from whom you can get references. Make sure that you notify them if they are to expect a call from your prospective employer and that they agree to give you a good reference.

❖ When you go on your interview, dress accordingly. You have a lot of competition, so you want to make a stellar first impression.

- ❖ Print out at least three copies of your resume on premium paper. One for you, and then at least two for your interviewers as there might be more than one.

- ❖ Establish rapport with your interviewer. Find something in common. Be personable and take part in the conversation. Remember, it is an interview for you as well to make sure this is the company for which you'd like to work. While you don't want to dominate the conversation, it's okay to ask questions, and even welcomed. It's great to be confident, but you don't want to appear overbearing.

❖ Once you leave, ask for their business card. Then, once you get home, send an email, politely thanking your interviewer for their time.

❖ Even if the interview went well, continue to look for other jobs and attend more interviews until you know for certain that you have been offered the job. Don't put all of your eggs in one basket.

Lesson 5-Work Hard/Play Harder

Have you ever watched a dog make fruitful attempts at attaining what they want? Do you notice their persistence?

With our dog Toffee, she mastered any trick to get a treat. The pup was as food-motivated as they get. When new people came to the house, she'd motion to the cookie jar in hopes they would catch on, slip her some food and she could capitalize on their generosity.

Brandi was toy motivated. She treasured her crate but wasn't confined to it. One day I came home to find her near her crate (which even I had trouble moving), and the crate was moved all the way across the floor in the middle of the room. Underneath that crate was Brandi's most treasured toy, clearly trying to "escape." I came to the analytical conclusion that Brandi must have pulled and pulled on that toy, dragging the crate in the process until I walked in the room. I have no doubt that had she kept trying; she would have freed her toy. Since I was there, I saved her the trouble.

Cuddles motivate Duke. This dog will lean up against anyone (he's not picky) and continually lean on them, (almost causing them to fall) until they bend down and hug him, kiss him, pet him...whatever they choose to do.

With Goldie, she also loves to snuggle but is adamant about getting the attention. If someone is sitting by her, she uses her snout to administer the biggest and most powerful nudge, urging them to pet her. If that doesn't work, her tiny but strong paws will slap them. She's hit me in the head before, demanding attention...or perhaps she was trying to knock some sense into me. I'm still not sure.

When all else fails, her lips puff out, her mouth puckers up and I know what's coming. That means she's lost all patience, and her only option is to bark or howl.

What do they all have in common? They work hard to get what they want, and then play harder afterward when they reap the rewards.

I have a day job, but my passion is writing. While I work hard at both, only with writing do I feel that I get to "work hard and play harder." While it is not easy to be a writer...and an indie writer at that, it is well worth it.

Of course, everyone has diverse passions and explores personal ways to play harder.

While my experience is with writing, I believe these following paradigms still apply.

When you first set a goal for yourself, it becomes a dream. It slowly develops into a passion. As you reach for the impossible, you'll find it's not quite the stretch you initially contemplated.

Whether you write blogs, books, articles, jingles, poems, create masterpieces, build houses, or fix things, you'll discover that either way, it's your passion.

With writing, you start with one work of creativity, and it turns into one hundred. Thousands of words.

You might notice when you first begin, you're able to type them out in rapid succession. They might appear as a spectrum of ideas that burst into view. Vibrant colors of a rainbow after a dark storm.

Your fingers desperately try to keep up with your mind as they beg you to slow down to take a much-needed break.

I can say from experience that although I can type over eighty words per minute, it never seems fast enough. No sooner than I complete one idea, dreams prompt another topic or a flowing paragraph. A pocket full of sticky notes with scattered scribbles and blurbs.

And as time progresses, the crest of the tidal waves eventually become even with the troughs, making way for a smooth flowing pattern. Things calm down.

As a motivation, sometimes I create my accolades or receive them from others and chase the next milestone. It can easily become a quiet obsession, a challenge, a quest to "put in my time" and see how much I could write. Would I grow tired? Bored? Would the seemingly never-ending well of enchanted ideas eventually run dry?

Does this sound familiar with anything in life?

There were days where I questioned my reasoning, justifying

my hours spent writing with the possibility to make money or find fulfillment.

But the real reason, in the beginning, was to prove to myself that I could do it. To see if I could rise to my challenges and chase my goals as a dog to its tail.

To my pleasant chagrin, I had written the stories that I set out to write and have published over fifteen books. While it won't grant me fame and fortune, it grants me peace of mind that I had accomplished what I had wanted. And the truth is, I don't want fame and fortune, although fortune isn't necessarily a bad thing.

So what this means is that with each article, book, poem or sentence, the writer learns more about writing. They polish their skills. They hone their craft. They find themselves connecting with people who share these same outrageous and time-consuming goals.

With writing, connecting to others urges each author to write more. All words stem from ideas that were incredibly similar or vastly different. The keys on the keyboard are doing what they were meant to.

For any and all authors, they have proven that they possess the stamina to write. The motivation to conjure up diverse and blossoming ideas, develop a story and put it out there for the world to see. A writer can keep the same format or experiment with different writing styles, tones, and characters. Change topics and shift gears. Go out on a limb and became daring with words and sentence structures. Anything and everything can become fair game to discuss. Develop a niche. And yes, rebel a little.

I might find that I'll write one thousand words a day. Heck on some days when I'm feeling ambitious, one thousand words can be written in an hour!

In a nutshell, as we take this fast-moving vacation through our life, we discover that so many possibilities present themselves directly in front of us. Often, we don't seize them because we don't believe we can do it, or we can't bring the project to fruition, or we don't have the time. Sometimes we convince ourselves that it isn't possible.

If you don't challenge yourself, however, you'll never know whether that is true or not. It's worth it to take a chance, set achievements for yourself and let the chips fall where they may. The only person stopping you, is well, you.

It's all about impassioned attitude, and that attitude is yours. Sometimes it takes a diligent work ethic, perseverance, sweat, anguish and maybe even tears. Sometimes it takes an insatiable hunger. Sometimes you need to push yourself harder than you've ever expected. There's always going to be obstacles, people getting in your way, dogs demanding to go for their third walk of the day in one hundred degrees weather...or zero degrees weather! These restrictions are part of life, but so are your dreams. If we find that we say "I can't do it" more often than not, then it might be time to change our attitude to one that says "I can."

Let's face it, if we make debilitating excuses, we'll believe them. If we give ourselves despairing limitations, we'll never surpass them. It pays to tap into our creativity once in a while. Raise the bar now and then and stretch our capabilities.

If you're a builder, don't think of only building a table as a small feat. Many of us can't even nail two boards together! If you're a writer, don't think of a sentence as only a drop in the bucket. Eventually, that bucket will overflow, and you'll be writing your fifth novel. Set a goal. Stick with it.   Work at it. Accomplish it. Before you know it, you'll be setting another one.

It's a lot of work, but since it's also fun, it enables you to work hard and play harder!

This rule doesn't only apply to writing. It applies to life.

You got this!

Lesson 6-Do What You Love and Don't Let People Tell You It's a Waste of Time

Dogs are notorious for doing what they love when they can do it. They don't hold back; they don't hide anything. They are transparent. They live for the moment and make their passion known, whether eating, playing, running in a park, or simply gathering their toys in one giant circle.

They simply do what they love and take some time to stop and just roll in the grass! And they don't care if anyone thinks it's a waste of time. Why? Because they enjoy it, they have fun, and it fulfills a small portion of their day.

Now, of course, dogs don't need to work, but they do teach us a lesson that even if you do not like your job one bit, it's important to roll in the grass once in a while...or, at least, partake in your version of fun!

Every person in this life has their definition of what is valuable and what is not. It's impossible for another person to dictate what's important to you in your life, in your story.

Has anyone ever told you that pursuing your dreams is not worth it, or muttered the words that it is a waste of time? I've spoken to some aspiring authors online over the past few years, some of whom have been deterred by naysayers warning them not to become a writer because they feel it is, essentially, a waste of time. I can only imagine how those words must've stung.

Without ever meeting these authors personally, I will say that those words "waste of time" piqued my ire quite a bit, as they almost squashed the dreams of someone who wished to try their hand at something pioneering. A refreshing beginning for which they have developed a passion and a vision for which they enjoy.

Each of us has our reasons for doing what we love. For authors, we might want to become rich or famous. We might want to leave our words floating around this earth long after we're gone. We might have an innovative message to convey, we might want to raise awareness about a specific topic, we might want to make an impression or we simply enjoy the creative license. We might enjoy the good old artist expression or some of the above or all of the above. We also might just want to break all of the rules and put long, run-on sentences in print. (Come on, just a little humor).

Since I started on this journey of writing and publishing a few years ago, it was anything BUT a waste of time. During that time span, I have accomplished goals that I set out to accomplish, and I've accomplished some goals that I didn't even know I should set!

What I Wanted:

When I first set out to write, my one objective was simple. Finish the book. That was it.

One straightforward goal for personal reasons. It was after I discovered the self-publishing sector that I decided to publish it, and then I took it a step further.

Of course, I wanted to make some money as I'd love nothing more than to write full-time, but I also wanted to donate a portion of the proceeds to animal rescue.

Since the moment I had published my first book, I've donated money, (and time) to animal rescue in addition to many donations of books and baskets to special events and fundraisers.

I plan to keep increasing that number the best that I can with each book that I write. My ultimate goal now? Have the means to help as many animals as possible with donations. But that's still a long road ahead. Maybe one day it will happen.

After writing for a while, I was greeted with a few pleasant surprises.

Over the years, I've received a great deal of emails from readers all over the world. Some have written to discuss my book. Others have written to tell me how much my first book, Finally Home: Lessons on Life from a Free-Spirited Dog, has touched them, and some have written to tell me that Finally Home inspired them to adopt a dog instead of shop for one.

Still, others have also written to tell me that they've donated money to animal rescue in honor of Buddy from Finally Home—a kind tribute that warmed my heart and brought joy to my soul.

Any writer will tell you that writing, while enjoyable, is a lot of work. Reaping rewards from that work is priceless.

Publishing is even more work. Formatting, designing book covers, editing, re-editing, creating trailers and marketing the book adds to the grunt work that goes into writing, especially for a self-published author. But I will say this, the fact that just one dog was saved because of my book, or that one person has donated to an animal rescue or even learned about animal rescue is a win-win. It's a tangible achievement.

With my series of Paw Prints in the Sand, people that had not recently been aware of puppy mills are now more informed and inspired to research the horror of puppy mills on their own. Sadly, what they will learn will be astonishing and unacceptable. But, there are very educated people out there who are uneducated about puppy mills and the horrific lifestyle that exists in those cramped up cages. My Paw

Prints in the Sand series sheds light on an otherwise very dim subject.

In addition to the kindness that others have paid forward in their way to animals, I've also met people from various rescue groups and have attended animal-rescue related events that focused on raising money for dogs. I've done book signings at some of these events and recently at a brick and mortar store; something that wasn't feasible in the beginning. Along the way, my network of animal-loving acquaintances and friends has increased immensely.

Fame isn't something I ever need, nor do I strive for it. Success, yes. But not fame, although I do respect those who have become famous. In fact, I've been fortunate to receive a short note from one of my favorite authors after sending him my book and have met some incredible people and artists who share the same affinity for animals.

Have I made millions? The answer to that is no, but that is okay. I've done what I can to raise awareness about animal rescue, and that is more than I ever thought possible. It's only a small contribution.

But a waste of time? It is anything but a waste of time. It is worth every moment of substantial hard work if just one life was saved. And if I ever do make a million dollars writing, my goal is to help as many animals as possible. Now, how is that a waste of time?

Following your dreams is anything BUT a waste of time. Isn't it worth it to make a small investment in yourself?

Other artists, craftsmen, hobbyists, and writers ultimately realize their goals. They have their reasons for writing and dreams they want to pursue. I hope they never let anyone demoralize them by convincing them they are wasting their time, and I hope they chase those desires with persistence, dedication, and passion.

You Can Do This!

We've all heard the clichés, "Life is too Short" or the one that contradicts it, "You've got your whole life to live!" In my opinion, both are true.

Life is too short. I can say this now as I'm in my forties. It seems like that with the blink of an eye; twenty years had passed.

How did all of those years disappear?

But then there's that other saying. "You've got your whole life to live." Well, it's true. You do. No matter what the age, you can never be certain when your time is near. Although this quote implies that our life may be a long one, all we know is that one day, it will be our time to leave this earth whether it's today or one hundred years from now.

Regardless, both clichés prompt the same question. Are you doing what you love?

Now when you first hear that question, it may mean different things to different people, and that's the point. It's open to interpretation. The important thing is, are you doing at least ONE thing that you love? Are you doing one thing that enhances your life?

Most of us have to work. Not all, but there are a lot of us who need to earn a living to pay our mortgage, buy food, gasoline, and countless other living expenses. We need to work to obtain extra money for entertainment or college education. The list goes on.

If you think about it, we spend at least forty hours a week at a job. Some spend more.

"Choose a job you love, and you will never have to work a day in your life." ~Confucius

Is it a job you love? Or is it one where you need to force yourself out of bed in the morning with enough time to give yourself a pep talk to get in the car and drive there?

If you've gone the first route of loving   your   job,   then congratulations! That is a good thing. A lot of people work jobs that they cannot stand. If you fall into the latter category, can you do something to offset it?

For instance, do you partake in a hobby that you do enjoy, such as bowling or golf? Is there a specific craft that you enjoy?

I'm a firm believer that there needs to be a balance. If you spend forty plus hours at a job you don't like, there should be some degree of happiness and pleasure in other areas of your life.

I work a full-time job, but I wouldn't label it as a passion. My passions lie elsewhere.

Writing, photography, hiking, dog-related activities- those are my passions. My happiness begins when I see my dogs' tails wag. Or when I have the chance to sit down and write, even if it is not a new book or blog. To me, that's relaxation time.

When I do concentrate on writing a book, it becomes a bonus. Writing and self-publishing novels have become enjoyable for a myriad of reasons. For one, I love the creating process. I love cultivating my ideas into full-blown stories. I enjoy "meeting" my characters for the first time. If they are of moral fiber, they have a charm of their own, but even the horrendous villains are close to my heart. I enjoy seeing them come to life, on paper of course.

Sometimes the plot development takes a while. I might not be sure where I want it to go, but then it happens. The entire captivating story unfolds before my very eyes. I not only know the middle but the ending as well. I realize where each character belongs and what their potential fate is.

The story is alive.

The second best part about writing is hearing from my readers. I've met wonderful people who have brought the characters to life in their minds, telling me why they love a character or hate them in my fictional thrillers.   And it's okay if they hate them. Hating the character implies that the character evoked some lucid emotion, and that's a good thing.

Along those same lines, getting feedback from my readers after they've read my non-fiction books might be the best part of the entire writing experience. Knowing that I've helped someone cope with loss or that my books have assisted someone in making a decision to adopt a dog is a sentiment that is unsurpassed!   It's a wonderful feeling to transition years of dreams into personal achievements!

Lesson 7-Have an Addiction, But Make it a Healthy One!

It's Tuesday. Time to Start Writing. Just like Wednesday, Thursday, Friday...you get the idea. :)

Can dogs develop addictions? I'd have to venture a guess and say that they can. Of course, they rely on us humans to feed that addiction.

Some may have a strong attachment to food as did my dogs, Toffee and Goldie. Some may find that they can't go anywhere without carrying around a toy, as did my dogs Duke, Buddy Thomas, Buddy Joe and Brandi.

Others have an addiction to their owners. Well, I might have to correct myself and say that all might have an addiction to their owners. After all, we are the ones that feed them, play with them and offer them our hearts from the moment we set eyes upon them.

But we can't fault them. Let's face it. We humans have quite an affinity for some addictive delights as well.

For each human, their addictions vary.

Some try to label it as a hobby. They start off slowly, carefully. They might even be cautious at first. Then, it escalates. The need becomes greater. Just a little isn't enough anymore. They can't wait to do it, and they don't have a choice.

Some love it, look forward to it and even if they try to stay away, they are sucked in like debris in a vacuum. They have to do it. If they aren't actively doing it, they are thinking about doing it. More than often, it consumes them. They might even sneak it once or twice. Other times, they make it through the day, but everything reminds them of it. A trickling touch of anxiety is nagging at them. A deep trance encompasses them for minutes at a time before releasing its hold, only to return moments later. Like an invisible monster, its tentacles wrapping themselves around the individual's thoughts, occasionally releasing themselves only to get a tighter grip.

They might try to stay away. They swear they will, even though they know they won't. Somehow, making idle promises out loud soothes them. As if they made the effort. As if they took a stand. They look around and see their tools and apparatus and try to look away, but they always give in, even if it is hours later.

Friends and family begin to notice that they look distracted. They can see the dark circles under their eyes from lack of sleep; a faraway look painted on their face as if they were visiting a remote island and they might very well be describing a lounge chair on their minds.

For others, they abhor it. Detest the remote possibility of doing it.

The very thought of it epitomizes torture in its most evil form. They wouldn't want to do it if their life depended on it. They don't want any part of it. They can't understand how others acquire such an obsession. Such an addiction. They don't feel sorry for them. They have no pity. They were never driven to try it. They never had the need. Never felt the compulsion. Their minds are tentacle free, and they like it that way. They'd be lying if they didn't see the results of what these individuals produce and if they said it didn't intrigue them, pique their curiosity, if even just a little bit. They still stay away and have no interest in trying it. After all, they have different vices for which to call their own.

I'm talking about that nasty little habit.   The one for which your teachers cautioned you.   The one some even tried to push on you, and then pushed a little harder. Encouraged you after class.   They might have even given you your first set of tools.   Stood by your side while they watched you do it.

Some parents might have even talked you into it.   They might've shown you how good it can be. Stimulated your interest.

It was habit that continued to form and grow and become something so enormous;   you couldn't get enough of it.

It's all about honing your creative genius. For some, I'm talking about writing.

It is one of those things that if you do love it, you can sit in a quiet or even not so quiet room, and let your fingers tap away without realizing how many hours have just passed. The hands on the clock keep racing around in dizzying circles while your creative mind lets ideas stream out into a screen in front of you. A state of consciousness exists but only focuses on the characters. The term tunnel vision applies solely to you. You might not have eaten for periods at a time. You might not have seen the sun set or the sun rise. Have you even blinked?

It's not a chore for those who love it. It's more of necessity. A drive. An obsession that inspires you. And just when you think you might close shop for the day, you receive another idea like an incoming nagging memo on a busy fax machine.

For hobbyists, I would imagine this desire didn't happen overnight. Heck, it might've even taken a few years. But there was always something there. You might've always been fascinated by interior design, or by cooking, or by building something, creating something fabulous, painting, drawing, dancing or whatever the "addictive" hobby might be.

For writers, there might have been stories formulating, ideas percolating, a cluttered mind full of heightened creativity with nowhere to go. Nowhere to be released.

Once you sit down in front of your desk, couch, or even your bed, you get the chance to unleash the words that have been scrambling in your brain like the numbers on a roulette wheel, except that writing isn't a game of chance.

Or is it?

Once you take your craft to the next level, once you take those manifested ideas and solidify them into a neat little package, is success a gamble?

It's a question I ponder and examine often. Can the best of dancers be hidden forever with no one to discover them? For writers, is it possible they are stuck in a world of poor marketing thus eluding success? On the contrary, can the most horrific of artists be successful just because of people they know, or the most terrible of writers with the most polished advertising techniques easily fly on the magic carpet of victory?

I believe in a world of karma. Fair things will happen to fair people, and hard work pays off. I also believe that triumph doesn't happen overnight.

When it comes to writing, it starts off as a hobby. Something to pass the time. Eventually, with any luck, it becomes a need. Something you not only want to do, but you have to do.

As you practice more, you improve more. With writing, you begin to notice your grammar changes, your spelling improves. Your punctuation is in the correct spot. Without question. You begin to get daring. Use "And" and "Because" at the beginning of a sentence. And it's okay. Because it fits and it works, and it makes a statement. And, don't look now, but you know what you're doing.

You've not only taken writing to the next level, but you've dusted it off, compounded any scratches and polished it. It not only looks clean but now it shines. You've made the transformation. You've taken a hobby and turned it into a modest craft.

While you have confidence, you know how you got where you are today. You know deep down how much hard work and dedication was put forth, and you don't take it lightly. It's a humble craft. One that screams that it needs attention and needs it often. And you're just the right person to oblige. You're just the right person to give it that attention and you do it well.

It is what you were meant to do. This same theory holds true for any craft.

And that's not such a bad secret addiction, is it?

Lesson 8-Find Your Passion

How do you find your passion? In my opinion, it's already there. It's something that you naturally enjoy.

I can give one example of when the happiness factor topped the charts...and it was the most simple thing in the world.

A picture.

A friend sent me a picture of a puppy that was up for adoption. She sent it to me for a very good reason.

It wasn't because I love dogs. And it wasn't because I wish that I could rescue all of them.

It was because it was a specific breed, a Nova Scotia Duck Tolling Retriever, which is rare to the town I lived in and she knew I was fond of them. While I admire puppies, I don't typically adopt them. I usually adopt senior dogs. And quite honestly we didn't have room for another.

But I was having a bad morning. The moment I saw his adorable little face, my heart melted. I forgot why I was so glum and moody. As natural as breathing, I knew I at least had to meet him. I emailed my friend to find out his whereabouts.

Nope, I didn't adopt him! But at that moment, I knew that the intense emotion of cheerfulness was something I should be experiencing more often. The kind of joy that occurs in an instant.

I can provide dozens of examples, but I think the message is clear. It's important to do what you love once in a while and find your passion. It would be fascinating to say that every day is a perfect day, but for most, that's not feasible. However, before you know it, you may say "I wish I did this or that" rather than "Remember when we did this or that?"

It's a difficult premise to follow but if you promise yourself to give yourself a day or even an hour a week to have some quality time for yourself, perhaps that grueling forty-hour work week won't seem so bad after all. With the hustle and bustle of everyday life, we lose sight of what is significant and things we promise to finish tomorrow, never get completed.

As I've gotten older, I've seen people close to me pass away, and I can't help but wonder if they enjoyed their life or if this profound realization ever hit them. *Was it too late*?

In my younger years, I was hesitant to do any of the things that I wanted to do unless I had someone who would join me. Looking back, I recognize how silly that was. You won't always find someone with the same interests. If you can't find someone, there is nothing wrong with going solo! Think of all of the activities you might miss out on just because you couldn't find someone to accompany you.

Just some food for thought from someone who realized in their forties that time doesn't stand still for anyone. Before I know it, another forty years are going to pass. Will I have done all that I set out to do? Will you?

In the words of a quote from my favorite "classic" movie, Shawshank

Redemption, "Get Busy Living or Get Busy Dying." It's those words that I memorize to remind myself to enjoy life, especially when I'm not feeling cheerful.

Is there something you enjoy doing every day? Hopefully, that answer is yes!

Moral? There is one. Enjoy your job. If you can't enjoy your job, find your passion and do something each day that you do enjoy. If you're creative, produce something even if no one will ever see it. You'll see it.

If you're handy, construct something. Smart? Invent something.

Have room for a pet? Adopt one! (Had to throw that in there, you know that, don't you?)

Do something that you enjoy. Once you accomplish your goal and find your passion, celebrate however you see fit!

Lesson 9- Show Compassion

And now...a short story for you.

When she first got into the car, she could hardly contain her excitement. She loved road trips. Usually, they went someplace awesome with dozens of hiking trails to explore. New scents and sights to discover. Afterward, she would go home to her castle, ask to go outside and take a refreshing dip in the built-in pool.

Today was a little different. The mood was somewhat somber in the car. No one said much, but that was probably because her parents had been fighting the previous evening. She didn't understand a lot of what they had said, but there was a lot of repetitive words, such as "shedding," expensive," baby." Oh, and the word "nuisance" came up a few times.

It was okay, though. Once they were out in the open air, surrounded by the prevalent sounds of nature, the arguments would stop, and the moods would be elevated. All would be right with the world.

The windows had been rolled down, and she could normally sense when they were getting close to the trail, but not this time. It felt as if they were going in a different direction. Perhaps there was a new hiking trail to discover. Either way, it would be fun.

The car slowed, and she bounced back and forth from window to window, trying to decipher where they were. She only saw a building, and not many trees surrounding it.

Her mom came around to open her door, and Trixie jumped out on command. As she went to wander off like she always did, her mom called her back to attach the leash to her collar. This was odd to her. She never needed a leash while hiking. She was smart enough not to wander off and never behaved badly in the presence of another human or dog.

She looked up at her mom, and now her dad was beside her. She was hoping for some praise or, at least, a pat on the head.

Instead, her dad spoke only to her mom. "Come on, let's get this over with. We have a lot to do today."

Her mom tugged on the leash, and Trixie followed closely behind, her eyes wandering to the new sights and then back toward the car. For some reason, unbeknownst to her, this place frightened her. She wanted to run back to the backseat of their vehicle and resisted moving forward. She knew this displeased her mom, but she didn't want to go.

"Come on Trixie. Stop pulling!"

Normally an obedient dog, the golden retriever gave in and walked slowly into the dreadful building.

Once inside, she got a sick feeling in the pit of her stomach, similar to the kind she got when it thundered outside. The echo of dogs barking, combined with terrified screams and yelps confirmed Trixie's fear that this place was no good. Thankfully she'd be leaving with her parents as soon as they finished their business here.

The woman at the counter looked at Trixie and Trixie slowly wagged her tail. The woman smiled slightly and focused her attention back on Trixie's parents.

"Reason for surrender?"

"We're having a baby and Trixie is too hyper. We also didn't realize how expensive it is to have a dog and with a baby on the way; there's just no room."

"Mmm, hmmm." The woman tapped away on a keyboard. "Age?"

"She's about nine years old."

"Allergies? Medications? Behavioral issues?"

"No."

"Please sign here confirming that you agree to surrender your dog. You understand that if she is not adopted, that this is a kill shelter. While we will do all that we can to find her a home, that might not be possible. Do you agree to these terms?"

Trixie looked up at her parents, still trying to determine what they were doing. She never heard the words "kill shelter" before.

Her dad answered the woman. "Yes." He then took a pen and signed the paperwork. Then, her parents did something she never thought they'd do. They patted her on the head and gave the leash to the woman behind the desk. As they left, they yelled "thank you" to the woman and walked out the door. Trixie thought she saw her mother crying.

"Wait! You forgot me!" Trixie thought. She barked and tried to lunge toward the door, but the woman's grasp was too strong.

"Come on girl. Let's get you into a cage."

She didn't understand where her parents went or why this woman was leading her into a room with dozens of barking dogs. None of them looked happy. Many had scooted to the back of their cages, some trembling and some had given into despair, their faces showing sadness so sorrowful.

Trixie went into her cage and yelped when the gate closed behind her. There was no bed, no pillows, no toys. Just a cold slab of cracked cement beneath her.

In the beginning, she stood by the gate of the cage, assuming her family would be picking her up shortly. Although she was never a complainer, she couldn't help but bark and whine every few minutes, just in case they had briefly forgotten about her.

When minutes turned to hours, and the slight trickle of sunlight turned to darkness, she retreated to the back of the cage, exhausted and panting. Her "cell mate" on the right bared his teeth every so often, so she made sure to steer clear of him and moved to the left, where a small poodle lay trembling and quiet in his cage.

They caught eyes and Trixie conveyed that she wasn't a threat. The poodle understood and wagged his tail one brief thump.

The place had a distinct stench. Aside from the normal canine smells, there was the smell of horror, sadness and even death. Trixie didn't like it there, and she figured none of the other dogs did either.

She longed to be in the comforts of her house, with her tennis ball, favorite duck and her lumpy, but comfortable bed.

Reluctantly, she fell asleep, hoping to wake up to her parents unlatching the cage in the morning.

When she slept, she dreamed. Her feet moved in constant synchronization with her elevated heartbeat. A howl from down the corridor woke her up, and she expected to find the gentle hands of her mother caressing her head, but instead, she looked up to see her neighbor peering at her. He looked like he hated her but she couldn't understand why. Maybe her dreams had woke him up.

She tried to go back to sleep, but she couldn't calm her racing heart. As the hours crept by, she became more and more agitated, looking for her parents.

This had to be some mistake. They should've come back for her by now. The only time she had been out of their care over the past nine years was when she visited her Aunt Sylvia down the road, but Sylvia had a dog Trixie's age who allowed Trixie to play with her toys, and there was also another bed for her. This definitely wasn't Sylvia's house.

By the time morning rolled around, Trixie felt a sharp pain on her back where she had been laying. She wasn't used to these accommodations. She woke up just in time to see a fluffy looking dog with a gray muzzle being dragged down the hall on a leash. He was walking slowly, a look of pure terror in his eyes. Trixie wondered where he was going. She heard the woman mumble something about "him being too old to adopt and that his time had come." She wondered what that meant.

Shortly after that, the woman came back with the leash, but the old-timer dog wasn't with her.

As a matter of fact, Trixie never saw the dog again and then she began to catch on.

It explained that smell of death that greeted her when she first walked in. The resident dogs have already come to know what that smell was, and now Trixie was privy to that information as well. She just didn't know what that dog did to deserve to die and wondered if she'd suffer that same fate.

After three days since she had last seen her parents, it felt like months. Her neighbor to the right stopped growling at her and instead now, just remained curled in a ball, getting up now and then to stretch before curling back up. He seemed unfazed by everything around him, unlike his demeanor when Trixie first met him. The energy he had demonstrated a few days ago diminished and Trixie had begun to feel the same way.

Some of the dogs were met by a smiling human who voiced the words, "we'll take him, or her." Trixie watched as some of the dogs were led out by a leash, their tails still tucked between their legs, but a tiny pep in their step as they made it through the front door and out into the fresh air.   Others weren't so lucky as they were led out to the back room, much like the old-timer she had witnessed on her second day in the facility.

A few humans knelt down next to Trixie's cage and, at first, she wagged her tail enthusiastically, but as the people walked away, claiming she was "just too old" she thumped her tail less and less.   She whimpered as she watched the younger, more energetic and spry dogs leave with a human. She only wished she could join them.

It was a Thursday when the same woman who brought her to her cage knelt down to the cranky male dog to her right. "Okay, Max. You gave it your best shot. We have to make room for some of the newbies." As if he knew, Max barked and writhed as the woman tried to leash him. He put up a good fight, but eventually the woman won. Although he was cranky, Trixie had grown used to his presence and watched as he, too, was led to the back room. She knew she'd never see him again and once again, she felt riddled with despair.

Within moments, after he was led out, a man Trixie hadn't seen before came in to wash out the empty cage.

Moments later, a young pit bull came running in, pulling on the leash and barking with joy. Apparently this young pup didn't have any clue about the journey she was going to embark upon. Perhaps she enjoyed being away from her family, or perhaps she never did have a family to call her own.

Trixie looked at her, and although she wanted to get up to meet her, she was too depressed.

It must have been a busy day at the shelter because cages were getting emptied of the "old stock" and replenished with "new." All of the barks, yelps, and whines that Trixie had gotten used to were replaced by new dogs, some who were excited and some who were just as nervous as Trixie.

She wished she could pacify them, but she had yet to pacify herself.

It had been days since she had any human contact, aside from the woman who poured food in her food bowl and water in the water bowl. Other than that, she hadn't felt the warm tenderness of the humans that she loved so dearly. She had forgotten what it was like.

The next day must've been a special day because the hallways were lined with a lot more people than had visited the previous days.

One by one, groups of families walked by, each examining the cages as they did so, some kneeling by a fellow dog and some skipping right over them.

Trixie caught eyes with a human who was not much taller than she was. She figured he was probably just as old.

The little boy looked at Trixie and with his parents oblivious to his lagging behind, he stuck his fingers in Trixie's cage, and she licked each one. He began laughing and did it again.

Trixie enjoyed the sound of his voice. It was gentle and soft. The little boy sat down and seconds later, his parents ran back afraid that he would stick his fingers in the wrong cage, but backed off when they noticed Trixie's tail wagging.

"Cody, you like this dog?"

Trixie went from a sit to a down and tried to give Cody her paw, but only got as far as it landing on the bars of the cage. The little boy put his hand on the pads of her feet, and once again Trixie kissed him. It was the most affection she had received in days and welcomed it with open paws.

Cody's parents knelt down next to her and stroked her head through the cage. The attendant asked if the family would like to play with

Trixie in a separate room, to which Cody's parents obliged.

Trixie couldn't contain her excitement. She was finally getting out of there. Maybe not with her original family, the one she truly loved, but with a family. That was all that mattered.

The attendant attached a collar around Trixie's neck, along with a leash and led her to the back into a little room. The room had some toys and a leather sofa. The sofa looked like it had seen better days, but Cody's parents sat on it while Cody sat on the floor ruffling Trixie's hair. Trixie loved the attention showed it by lavishing the little boy with sloppy dog kisses and the boy giggled.

"Mommy, can we please keep her? She loves me!"

"No, I'm afraid not Cody. We just wanted to look today. They'll be other dogs."

"But I want THIS one!"

"Cody, we have things to do today, and we have vacation next week. If she's still here after that, then maybe."

Cody's parents ignored his cries as they signaled the attendant to retrieve the golden retriever.

"Alright, Cody. We have to get to that birthday party. Say goodbye to your furry friend."

Through tears, Cody knelt down next to Trixie and kissed her on the head. Trixie reciprocated by nestling her head against his face. She whined as she was pulled away yet again by the attendant as she only wanted a family to call her own and yard to run and play, and even a friend like Cody to play with. Instead, she was placed into her lonely and cramped cage with no one to give her attention.

Maybe one day her family would return for her, realizing they made a mistake. But that day never came.

This story is very true, except with different names and different breeds. All too often dogs (and other pets) are abandoned, neglected, painfully waiting for their owners to come back, or at the very least, to gain a new family, but for far too many, new families never come.

Each and every day, dogs (and other animals) are left to fend for themselves. It doesn't matter what the reason as sometimes, there isn't a viable one. They are animals, yes, but those animals love deeply, and they grow attached to their families. They are a lifetime commitment and should be treated as such. They can't possibly comprehend why the people who they had loved the most are no longer taking care of them.

It takes a special someone to be this pet's savior. Having compassion for these pets makes a world of difference for them. It gives them a chance to love again, to move forward with their new lives and become comfortable and joyous in a new home, living out the rest of their years.

If we can dig deep into our hearts to find compassion for those who need it, more often than not, that animal's life will radically improve. This same theory is extended toward people as well. Showing just a minimal amount of compassion can go a long way and all it takes is a conscious effort and a keen awareness of what is occurring in the world around us!

Lesson 10-Exercise Tolerance

After Buddy Junior had passed away, we were contacted by a rescue group to let us know that there was a dog, named Duke, who needed a home for the Holiday weekend. He was eight years old, recently got neutered and had many teeth pulled.

The only problem was that he was at the veterinarian's office and wasn't eating. We couldn't pick him up until he showed an appetite.

Five days later, he began to eat, so we got the green light to collect him.   At first sight, we knew something was wrong with him as he was eight years old and showed no enthusiasm, laying on the tile floor at the veterinarian's office, alert but languid.

After numerous vet visits before even adopting him, we discovered he had Lyme Disease.   Many medications and eight weeks later, we adopted Duke, and his Lyme Disease was cured!

During that time, he was too drained to move.   However, our other dog Toffee was up and about and curious about her new friend. So, every day she nestled up on his blanket next him, despite his growling and protests, and randomly, she'd lean toward him and kiss his eyes.

He hated it. He couldn't get up, but he'd warn her with a growl, for which she'd look away, but still wouldn't get up and move away from him. It was clear she was in awe of him and felt comfortable right next to him.

Day in and day out, she'd carry on this routine, laying by him, kissing his eyes and face and...he'd growl.

By the end of the first week, when Duke had a little more strength, but not much, he began to loosen up at the sight of Toffee approaching and knew what was coming next. Of course, it was kisses from his new friend, except now, he didn't protest.

For the two years, they were together before Toffee passed away, they became the best of friends, with Duke tolerating his daily (or hourly) kisses from Toffee, never once growling at her again.

What happened? He developed tolerance and sought after Toffee when she wasn't near him. He started to lay by her, using her back as a pillow and didn't mind any kisses from her from that point on.

In life, it's not always easy to develop tolerance, however, sometimes it's necessary, and we might even welcome the result afterward. Toffee was trying to be friendly and fell in love with Duke from day one. Although he might not have been completely comfortable in the beginning, his tolerance toward her (and her persistence) deemed them the closest of friends.

Often, everyday situations get under our skin, and we feel like we are going to explode if they don't cease. Tolerance is the furthest thing from our minds.

But, often understanding why certain actions are taken can help us become more tolerant of it and even though it requires patience, the end result is becoming less frustrated and possibly even more understanding.

Lesson 11-Make Connections. Make Friends. Treat 'Em Well

In 2014, my little angel, Toffee made her journey to the rainbow bridge after suffering a fatal seizure. The loss of Toffee was heartbreaking. Although she was quite a handful, her daily antics, and the role of my shadow was something for which I had grown accustomed. Losing her knocked the wind out of my sails.

Six months later, just when I thought I was learning to cope, we lost Brandi. She was almost fourteen years old. She was the only dog that we didn't rescue, however, to give credit where it is due; she is the one who rescued us.

She was the quiet presence that calmed the storm. The Alpha for all of our dogs. The one who lived with us the longest, and owed us nothing yet gave so much.

Brandi was composed under all circumstances. Each picture of her displays the same resemblance. Cool, stoic, unexcitable. Even when a dog attacked her on her walk, she laid down without a whimper as I worked on pulling the dog off of her. (Thankfully, she only suffered a scratch and I only suffered a bigger flesh wound).

She was the dog who welcomed any other dog into the household without hesitation, but who trained them to behave with her low growls and limits to what she allowed them to do.

With each dog we adopted, they tested her patience and without biting any of them (well, not seriously), she taught them who was in charge. They could play with their toys whenever they wanted. Her only rule—just don't touch hers. They could eat their food, and she wouldn't bother them; just don't rush her while she's eating and don't try to take from her bowl. Once she set the ground rules, every dog followed and lived in a peaceful, cheerful existence.

Almost every time dogs meet for the first time, there is a challenge for alpha, and she won each time.

It was amazing how one dog— who was not even that big, and smaller than our males— was able to keep everyone in check, and even befriend them in the process.

Dogs appreciate having an alpha in their life as it calms them and assures them that their alpha has everything under control. They needn't worry. That's the first step for them to become friends.

People operate a little differently. Most don't want to relinquish control and in reality, an "alpha" friend who always tries to dominate situations, might not be a true friend.

I believe that's why it's important to find friends who share common interests, who have your best interests at heart and who don't want to control you. Instead, they simply want to be your friend!

From a young age, I've been taught that if you have one good friend that you can count on through thick and thin, one that will stand up for you, cry with you, laugh with you and try to guide you when the chips are down—then that one friend is all that you need.

Throughout life, I've been blessed and have to say I've had a lot of great friends. As I've gotten older, I've been a little more selective and have weeded out any of the bad from the good.

I think it's all about perspective. Some people need to have a lot of people to rely on, so they thrive on having as many friends as possible. I suppose it all depends on your individual needs.

I've had "friends" who have worn the best friend label, only to find they would stab me in the back in a moment's notice. Those friends have lightly been kicked to the curb, and my life has been drama free since that moment! I believe you'll know when a friend is becoming an emotional vampire, sucking the life out of you. When it's all give and no take, that's symptomatic that something is incongruous. And if they stab you in the back as well?

Then it is time to say goodbye and move on. Nothing is worth a back-stabbing.

What if You Have a Different Lifestyle?

With many of my best friends, as we've grown older, we've moved away, lived dissimilar lifestyles, followed diverse career paths, but yet we are still as close as ever.

I chose not to have children and rescue dogs instead while all of my best friends are raising a family.

Do we have different choices to make? Yes! Different battles to fight? Of course! But we are still there for each other and give advice to the best of our ability. It doesn't mean we've grown apart. It merely means we've grown up.

It's not about quantity of friends. It's about quality. Find someone who has your best interests at heart. You don't need to have a people pleaser as a friend; they will turn on you on a dime. You need someone who will stand up for you and believe in you. Someone who will encourage you when you are chasing your dreams and snap you back to reality when you decide to go to the dark side.

You don't need someone who is going to judge or ridicule you. Those people are easy to find. And you don't need a friend who is bossy or over-needy or that "alpha" friend.

And when you build your circle of friends, hold on tight and treat them well. One hand washes the other, and when you have friends you can count on, who can also count on you, life becomes just a wee bit easier and bearable.

If you find that one good friend, it's okay to give 110% of your efforts because you know they will do the same for you. There shouldn't have to be a scorecard, and you know that friend will be there for you no matter what the circumstance.

And, if you can't find one that suits your needs, there are plenty of dogs in the shelters who would be more than happy to be that friend!

Does Technology Affect Personal Relationships?

Technology has come a long way over the past ten years and with it, relationships and the method of socialization have changed as well.

I find myself in awe as I look back at the late nineties. While it seems like that was ages ago, in truth, I still remember it like it was yesterday.

The technological age as we know it was basic and trite, to say the least.

It seems at that time, computers were just introduced as a household item, and the Internet was something that only some businesses possessed. If you did have the Internet at home, it was most likely a dial-up connection. Gasp! Did I just say dial-up? Thankfully, we've come a long way.

At the same time, cell phones were a luxury for those who could afford them. Data packages weren't even available at that time. Beepers seemed to have been commonplace, and pay phones were still on every corner.

Fast forward to the year 2016 and technology has advanced tremendously. Not only does almost every household have one computer, but almost every person in that household has their own.

Telephone land lines—the ones attached to a wall with a phone wire—are few and far between and even if one exists in the home, it's almost a guarantee that all occupants have their own cell phone—even young children!

Along with the technological revolution, social media has become the new norm, and people have found new ways to connect. Many of them are useful for a variety of reasons, such as to connect with old friends, advertise or as a means of a professional tool to develop an employee/employer search function or relationship.

Though we've taken part in this new social aspect, I often feel that touching base with humanity is at an all time low.

Start with the young child on the block. It is rare that you see children riding their bicycles, playing kickball or dragging their Barbie doll camper out into the middle of the lawn, using their imagination to spark creativity. No longer do they knock on their friend's doors or simply walk into their friend's house like we did as kids.

Even video games are played with another person without even leaving the house, or without being in the same state for that matter!

Conversations can take place via Instant Messenger or Skype, never once hearing the other person's voice.

You can download a library of books within sixty seconds, a collection of music, movies, and video games, chat with the rest of the world and furnish your entire living room without ever leaving your house or speaking to anyone over a telephone connection. You can even see the person you are speaking to by using a webcam— something we only imagined in the eighties and is now a common reality!

We have a world of convenience right at our fingertips, so how can this be a dreadful thing?

Successful Communication

All of the modern day luxuries provide a plethora of economically sound and expedient opportunities.

While we have come a long way, there are some areas which can use improvement.

When using online sites as the main source of communication, the misunderstandings and downfalls occur in a few different areas:

Tone, Facial Expressions, and Body Language

Hiding Behind a Facade

False Identity

In the face-to-face real world, we are given some distinct advantages when we communicate. For one, we can hear the tone in each other's voice. In a text, email or a post on someone's Facebook wall, something that might have been said in a joking manner can easily be misconstrued as offensive.

Another thing we lack is viewing facial expressions and body language. When we sit down at a table together and have a live conversation, we read each other's body language and facial expressions. Even though no one has ever sat us down and explained this to us, we are taught from a young age how to interpret body language in others. These are two more things that are lacking in this new age of conversation.

Also, there are the possibilities of false identities. Although more websites require, at the very least, a login, some allow essentially anyone to comment on a blog or a forum. Sometimes, people can write whatever they can get away with, not caring who it hurts in the long run.

Along those same lines, since in essence, we are all hiding behind the monitors of our computers, we can say or do anything we want with minimal repercussions.

Often, respect and manners fly out the virtual window.

Etiquette

Many of us have read Emily Post's book on social etiquette, but now the entire playing field has changed. There's a new etiquette in town, and that is the modern era of Social Networking.

In this day and age, where we live in an "anything goes" society, etiquette, and social grace or manners are easily forgotten. Often they are replaced with those of inconsideration or callousness.

It seems since we can easily hide behind the mask of a computer, we no longer have to abide by the rules of society. People are thrilled to have their opinions heard and in many cases, that is a good thing. There are a lot of people out there who have oodles of knowledge that they can share with the rest of the world, and some of it is invaluable.

Shouldn't we, therefore, abide by what we've already practiced in the real world and still have respect for each other, even though we'll never see each other face-to-face and most likely never have a conversation on the phone?

I've seen more arguments on social media than I've seen in the time I've been on this earth.

I've witnessed more strangers take a stab against someone they've never even met just because they could. They have courage behind that computer.

Then there is cyber bullying, which is a tragedy for anyone, but especially for young kids today. How is a teenager supposed to live their carefree years having fun if there will be live footage on YouTube the next day?

While the Internet is a blessing in many ways, I can only hope that we don't lose sight of empathy and compassion towards others, whether or not we disagree with them.

There is such a way to disagree respectfully, and I can only hope that one day, there is a book on Social Networking Etiquette (little plugin for those who want to write it)!

Lesson 12-Relax!

Oh, it's not easy. Believe me. I am one of those people who have to work hard at relaxing. Sitting down to watch a television program is something I have to talk myself into and convince myself that it is okay to unwind for a little while, even though the dishes haven't been washed. "It's okay to miss a day of exercise or not clean the house. The tilted picture frame on the wall? That can wait. Sit down and watch one show!!"

That is the conversation I have with myself nearly every time I try to relax. I've gotten so used to a hectic lifestyle, that it is second nature. Relaxation is foreign to me.

There is nothing wrong with relaxation, however. As I was writing this book, I had been sitting in my single chair recliner for over three hours, while my dogs slept lazily on the floor and couches. Just when I felt that my eyes had glazed over, my one dog, Duke, gave me no warning and jumped in my lap. Now, remember it's a single chair recliner, laptop in hand and a seventy-pound dog on my lap. Not an easy task to juggle trying to save my work and find a safe place for my laptop.

A part of me wanted to move and finish writing, but within mere minutes, Duke was fast asleep, snoring and completely at ease. What did he make me do? Settle down and unwind.

Hesitantly, I put the laptop on the floor, wrapped my arms around Duke, tried to get some feeling in my legs after a while of him laying on me, and enjoyed the moment. I realized that one day after Duke is long gone, I would cherish that snuggle more than anything.

The body needs to loosen up, so there is nothing wrong with taking some time out for yourself once in a while, putting the chores away and just simply sitting idle to let the feelings of calmness all soak in. Recharging the batteries, so to speak, so that when you are ready to tackle the world, you can do so fully rested.

It's ironic how as you grow older, things change, including the way that you have programmed yourself to think. It's expected of course. How can your thoughts not change? With age, comes maturity. And with maturity comes wiser decisions and more deft emotions than when you were in your teens.

At least, we hope so.

What is it they say? "We're not older, just more seasoned and more experienced." As adults we're supposed to live by those words, aren't we? Set an example for those following in our footsteps.

So while it's natural to grow older, wiser and more experienced, I believe a lot of what shapes us is the memories we make while we were younger. But what we don't realize is that we should make more memories as adults.

From age sixteen, I've worked continuously, sometimes combining work with attending school and sometimes I worked two jobs.

The goal? To make money of course. The reality? Time was rushing by and always does.

When in your twenties, it probably seemed that you had the energy to work and still have time to go out and have fun. We may think that everything will remain the same, and we will have plenty of time for everything.

As we get older and establish more responsibilities, it seems we only have the time to work, not realizing that the world around us is changing. Not realizing that time stands still for no one.

Or perhaps we do realize, but don't have time to stop and smell the roses...literally.

It seems like an uncomplicated concept, really, but I never truly understood the magnitude of slowing down until I was out of work for two months.

The awakening, or perhaps a better word is an epiphany, happened after I had lost my job following September 11th.

After all of the overwhelming heartache our nation had just endured, I used the two months to reflect and catch up on things for which I never made the time.

If you lived in New York at the time, you might have remembered that September 11th fell on one of the most stunning days of the year. The sky was maritime blue; the humidity was minimal. It was diametrically opposed to the tragic events of that day.

The rest of September's weather followed suit.

Nothing could diminish the solemn grief that followed those sorrowful days. Even if you didn't know someone personally that had passed away, you couldn't help but feel sympathy for the families that did.

There were no appropriate words that could be spoken to make sense of what happened. I don't believe such words will ever exist.

All you could do was move on to the best of your ability and that is what I had tried to do.

Even though I was temporarily unemployed, I made it a point to wake up each day at the same time as if I had a job to attend. I didn't want to get in the habit of sleeping late and being unproductive. I didn't want to let depression sink in.

Instead, I created a regimen for myself consisting of three main philosophies:

Health, Mind, Work.

- Exercise in the morning for good health

- Learn during the day to sharpen the mind

- Complete chores at night to remain in a "work" routine

Here's where I realized the importance of stopping to be grateful for the little things in life and even slow down a little.

And indeed, the best things in life are free.

In the mornings, I began my exercise routine by strolling around the neighborhood. Eventually, since I didn't have to rush anywhere, there were moments my brisk walk slowed to a leisurely walk.

Exercise is often thought of as having to be fast-moving to benefit from it.

While that is somewhat true to slim down, there's another benefit you can gain while moving at a slower pace.

You gain the opportunity to look around you. To see things you might've only previously skimmed over or glanced at without taking a minute to see details.

When was the last time you saw the slight variance of color in a rose? Was it a ravishing red or candy apple? Perhaps it was sunrise yellow or bubblegum pink. Have you ever sat on the sand at the beach to watch the actual bubbles from a wave that has just broken on the shore? We've all seen birds making a nest on the nature channel, but when was the last time you ever actually watched one from a few feet away?

It is these simple things that we take for granted.   They are there every day for us to observe and get pleasure from, but we simply don't have the time or possibly don't even know what we're missing.

During that time, my exercise expanded from simply walking around the neighborhood to walking at the beach or around the park.   I had plenty of time to reflect.

How sad it is that we travel through life with our eyes open, but do we ever truly see?

Perhaps my modified thought process had caused me to gain a new reverence for nature due to the events of 9/11.

It could also be in part because I realized how quickly our life can pass us by, or more tragically, how unexpectedly life can be taken from us. No notice, no chance to say goodbye, no possibility of seeing or doing things one last time...or for the first time for that matter.

We spend our days at work because we have obligations. To live, we need money. We want to buy materialistic things that are marketed to make us believe they will, in turn, make us happier.

But is that truly the case?

Life doesn't slow down for anyone, and the proficient hands on the clock keep turning no matter how hard we try to slow it down.

We owe it to ourselves and taking a day to reflect can be just what we need. Sometimes we forget this, so I'm just writing this as a friendly reminder.

Walk along the shore, hike a mountain, sit in the backyard without a telephone or television interrupting precious thoughts. There's a quiet, lesser-known peacefulness and enjoyment that goes hand-in-hand with the appreciation of the little things in life. If you stop and take a look around, you may realize that you may get the same satisfaction from sitting atop a mountain with your legs hanging free, listening only to the sounds of the birds chirping or a steady waterfall versus watching that big screen television with the various sounds blasting from the speakers.

Just make sure you don't get too close to the ledge!

Lesson 13-Tweak the Rules

Each time an author vows to take a break from writing, the flood gates open and ideas pour in, challenging the author to lift up their pen and break those vows yet one more time.

Elizabeth Parker Books
www.elizabethparkerbooks.com

In certain areas of our life, there are rules we have or want to abide by each and every day.

There are some rules that I follow adamantly with regards to training dogs...and some, well, some I break now and then.

My primary goal is to make sure all dogs get along for the most part. Any slight disagreements between them, I aim to nip in the bud immediately.

I attempt to make them obey when I give a command, walk safely on a leash, play nicely and take treats gently.

My first official adopted dog, Buddy Senior, loved to jump on people. It was an exceptionally difficult habit to break, and he was an extremely venturesome, friendly, yet powerful dog. Since those days, I discourage my new adopted dogs from jumping.

Well, all except one. Goldie was adopted last year, and she is a sixty-pound golden retriever—all heart but loves to play.

She also has one habit that some might not appreciate. She LOVES to hug. She jumps up on random people, wraps her paws around their waist (if she can reach their waist) and nestles her head against them. It's endearing and beautiful to watch. Now, I know I should stop her, and I do if it's a complete stranger she's trying to hug (yes, she's tried). However, when it is me she is hugging, I can't, no matter how hard I try, push her off of me. I simply hug back.

What did I do? I broke one of my cardinal rules—no jumping. It just goes to show, however, that sometimes, rules can be broken...and sometimes it's acceptable!

In our lives, sometimes, it's suitable to break the rules as well...as long as we're not hurting anybody!

My rule breaker happened with writing. I remember the day. I've heard that it happens to other people. They talk about it and write about it, but the idea seemed so far-fetched that I couldn't imagine it would happen to me.

I had been having a week chock full of mixed emotions. I'd been having frustrations at work and a lack of sleep. There were goals I had wanted to reach, mixed with goals I was accomplishing, topped with more goals added to the list. At the same time, I was experiencing excitement, anticipation, and hope for a new venture.

I had been plugging away hard at work all week with writing, marketing, and photography, so I didn't know when it would happen or if it would happen, but that morning my fears were confirmed.

It happened.

That morning was the day I woke up, looked around and said, "so this is what it feels like."

It was the day I had lost my momentum. The hamster on the wheel of creativity had died right in front of me. Nothing left but a shell of what might've been and a stream of empty thoughts flowing into a river going nowhere.

Time seemed to stand still for a minute. Thoughts were moving in slow motion. Like the grainy film of yesterday's reels, nothing of relevance was coming to mind.

I opened my laptop in hopes of some free association writing.

Perhaps my fingers would type what my mind wouldn't think. It didn't happen. I wound up surfing the Internet to repetitive sites, none of which I had intended on visiting. It was all by habit. Not one of the websites could keep my interest long enough to read what was on the page.

My dog began whining, hinting for me to entertain her and I reluctantly got up to take her for a walk. My morning walk is something I normally enjoy, but I dragged my feet the entire way.

And then it hit me like a bat to a ball.

Plain and simple. The house was in disarray, and I hadn't slept. Put the two together and it caused a major meltdown in my creativity. I suppose the Feng Shui of my mind was completely misaligned.

I should've known. To become productive or enthusiastic in any area of my life, the environment around me needed to be in order. I'd guess that is symptomatic of Obsessive-Compulsive behavior but at the same time, everywhere that I looked, I didn't see ideas. I saw chaos. I saw a new item added to my mental list of things to do.

It is my belief that many of us undergo a time in our life when we are not motivated. Whether it's writing, exercising, working, or even watching a movie, if our thoughts are elsewhere, it becomes next to impossible to focus on anything.

The trick is finding out what is blocking our mind from being constructive. Recognize the source of that blockage and fix it or at least, find a way to make some headway in getting it rectified.

Staring at the problem will not resolve it. All it will do will further the lull in productivity and increase anxiety and tension.

In my situation that morning, the resolution happened to be a simple one. Straighten up the house and run necessary errands.

So why was it so difficult to get it done?

The answer is simple. I wanted to write, so I tried to focus on writing. All that did was waste two hours of my day when I could've taken care of other pressing responsibilities and then save the writing for later.

Other conflict resolutions might not be as effortless. So what are we to do when chaos busts open the door and enters our life?

Life is going to throw us tragedies and for those, all the planning in the world might not be able to help. For the rest of life's issues, however, there are certain things we can do.

As we go about our day, the chances are that every so often we'll say, "I've got to fix that" or "I have to pay the bills" or "I have to call Aunt Millie."

All of these worries and concerns build up in a compartment of our mind and eventually start taking up space, much like a nagging relative, leaving little room for anything else to manifest there. As you try to become creative or motivated, those little nagging relatives tap us on the shoulder and say "don't forget to do this" or "did you make that phone call yet?!"

Developing a thought process becomes close to impossible.

There will be things we can't get to right away, so what I find helps is to create a list.

Use your smartphone, sticky notes, napkin...whatever you can get your hands on and start recording what you have on your mind. Don't limit it to things you have to do. Include your worries, concerns, fears or anything that is weighing on your mind. Put it in front of you and then kick those nagging relatives out of your head. Don't worry, they won't get insulted, and they'll be sure to return soon.

Don't Become Your Own Worst Enemy

The lack of productivity on those days was prompted by a goal I had set about adhering to a schedule of writing. Due to my stubborn nature, I became my own worst enemy.

To conform to my rules, I didn't want to bend. I was going to be dedicated, proactive, and stick to my daily itinerary come hell or high water.

Guess what? It didn't happen. So what did I learn?

Tweaking the Rules is Acceptable!

Making a schedule and devoting myself to it is a normal necessity in my professional life. In my personal life, however, I am more apt to fly by the seat of my pants than plan anything. What I've learned is that there are going to be times when it is suitable to let the two worlds collide. Sometimes I'll need to plan in my personal life, and sometimes my work schedule will have to be modified.

Things are going to come up. Errands need to be run and sometimes deadlines aren't met. That's life.

There are exceptions to every single rule and if every so often they need to be broken, then so be it.

And then resume life as normal!

Lesson 14-Break from the Norm

Since raising dogs, I've noticed that they love to conform to a routine. They know what time they are having breakfast, dinner, and usually, they know the time that I will take them on walks or play.

I don't always get the opportunity to take them to the park, but on days when work is not so demanding, and the weather is cooperating, I open the car door, let the dogs in and venture on down to the park as a little surprise for them. And guess what? They love it! Their excitement is apparent as they sit by the window in the car, wondering where we are headed. Now and then, I'll hear an animated whimper and then when we arrive at our destination, their tails are wagging, and they are in their glory. Observing their happiness is enough to make my day as well.

Sometimes it's good to break from the norm. Not just for dogs, but for people too!

Do you find that sometimes you wish to break from the norm in your life? Perhaps you wish you were a little more courageous, or that you were a bit more of a daredevil?

Or are you the opposite? The type that is always being told to slow down and be careful?

Risks are going to present themselves throughout everyone's lifetime. In elementary school, the biggest risk you are presented with might've been whether or not to climb a tree. In high school, most teens are scared to approach a member of the opposite sex. Once you make your way into the working world, learning a job presents a risk, as does getting promoted or leaving one job for another.

Some people are happier with their feet planted firmly on the ground, never traveling that extra mile to witness what is just around the bend, while others prefer to soar through the skies, taking risks and letting the chips fall where they may. Some enjoy the excitement.

Personally, I'm somewhere in the middle. I like to be able to see the pebbled ground beneath me, however, if the reward is worth it, I'll go ahead and take the plunge to do something that might chase me out of my comfort zone.

That's not to say I will enjoy being out of my comfort zone if any uncertainty exists (which usually accompanies risk) but once I see the results, providing they are positive, I'm glad I skipped testing the waters and dove in feet first.

Now, this only goes for risks that won't necessarily get me killed. You won't see me skydiving by choice, hang-gliding, or wrestling alligators anytime soon. I won't even ride a roller-coaster unless someone has very impressive coercion skills. That's only happened a handful of times, and I doubt it'll happen again. Something about not having control of an extremely fast bucket-like-chair scares me a little.

So, in everyday life, why take a risk? Why deviate from the norm? What's the benefit and reward?

It all depends on how much you are willing to lose. So, if you're planning on opening a business and need to take out a loan and lay out the money, you stand to lose all of that money. But, if the business succeeds and does well, then it wasn't all for naught. You will be doing something that you love.

In the past few years, I've tried a few different "risks" with changing jobs and career paths entirely, and while they could've been successful, I wasn't chasing my dreams.

So, in 2010, I took another risk when I began writing.

Was I scared? Well, I wouldn't say scared. I was apprehensive. I didn't know anything about the world of publishing. I didn't know what to expect or if I would succeed. Even though it was only a few years ago, it seems there wasn't as much information on self-publishing as there is now. I had no idea how to format books, book covers and lastly, I didn't even know how to promote my books! I was completely wandering out of my comfort zone!

Even with some apprehension, it was fun. Everything about writing was new and stimulating and still is. I'm sure other authors will agree. If you love doing something, then it does not even feel like "work" in the traditional sense of the word.

Today, I'm happy that I decided to go for it. While the first year was rocky, I stayed with it, learned, persisted, researched and learned some more. It is safe to say that if you're passionate about something, do everything in your power to make it work.

And that's exactly what I did.

I did what I thought was right, made some mistakes along the way, fell, picked myself up, brushed myself off and began writing again.

Sometimes the best ideas need time to become part of the big picture. Don't rush into anything and always weigh all of your options. Anytime you break away from normal life, as with any risk, you'll never know until you try. But there might just be a reward after all.

Lesson 15-Learn from Your Mistakes...and then Move on Without Regret

That growling. That yapping. That panting. The jumping and obscure, worrisome barks that accompany certain doggy meetings.

Dogs sometimes clash. Just like people, not all dogs will like each other and get along. Providing no one gets hurt, however, a dog will usually leave their fight, perhaps somewhat shaken, but then shrugs it off hours later. For the most part, they will still return to the same dog park and will probably still even make friends with other dogs. They don't sit and ponder the past. Dogs are creatures of the moment. Most likely, they will learn from their mistakes and will avoid their opponent dog if they ever encounter them again but they don't become bitter against life and everything in it.

They don't regret leaving the house that day. They just move on. Regrets are not a word in their vocabulary.

Wouldn't it be nice if people were able to do the same?

"A man is not old until regrets start taking place of dreams." ~ Anonymous

Above is a quote that I read somewhere that hit home and caused me to have one of those moments where I'm forced to sit and ponder. I'm not sure where it originated, but its meaning holds true.

We all have done or said things that we wish we could take back, but hopefully, we learned from our previous errors, and that is the important thing. Life is about learning lessons and moving on.

The moral of this is to make a positive change and accomplish the things that have been put off. It doesn't have to be big, but if it is something that nags you on a daily basis and is positive, why not do it?

After all, there's still time to accomplish your dreams and at least, dispose of regrets if even on a small scale.

Regrets are pointless.

As you roam through your life, on a particularly good day, you may say that you have no regrets, but feel quite the opposite if life is not cooperating as you had hoped.

Some may even go as far as to say that they regret major life decisions that they have made. Even though we don't always get what we want when we want them, there's usually a good reason for it. There are times when the thing you want the most, turns out to be something you did not want after all and the thing you didn't want, turns out to be your most prized, treasured possession.

Though life might not go according to plan, I don't think regret is a safe word to use. You can't change the past, but you can take small steps to alter the future to be a positive one without any regrets.

Lesson 16-Appreciate Those Who Have Helped You!

Elizabeth
Parker
Books

There's nothing like getting love from a little puppy who looks at you with eyes of innocence like you are the best thing since sliced bread.

With senior dogs, that look is tenfold. There is an appreciation factor that comes into play as they realize you have made a commitment to love them—with their gray hair, bad teeth and all—for the rest of their furry lives.

It's true they make it easy, but their appreciation is notable. We know they appreciate us just as much as we appreciate their exquisite presence in our lives.

Appreciation is something that should be shown once in a while, as people might not realize how much you treasure them. That holds true for parents, grandparents, children, friends, significant others and everyone in between.

My biggest appreciation is my childhood, family, and my mother. I am happy to say that I have great memories of my younger years. Despite my father's life ending way too early, the rest of my days were spent with immediate family, extended family, those we considered family and close friends.

Our summers were spent in above-ground pools, barbecuing, eating sandwiches and Entenmann's cakes (which, I still love by the way).

My neighborhood was incredible. All original owners were married when they bought their houses, and each had a bunch of kids—all that were about the same age. Most of whom I still talk to today!

We lived on a cul-de-sac, so the word "traffic" never meant a thing to us as cars rarely even came down our block, probably because no one knew it was there.

The rest of the days were spent playing kickball, red light, green light one-two-three, Barbie dolls, Frogger and riding our bikes for endless hours up and down the block. Occasionally we ventured off to forbidden places, but let's keep that our little secret.

My best friend and I were not adverse to collecting bugs (eoowww), dressing them up and then letting them go. Yeah, we dressed up bugs.

So, why am I telling you all of this? There is a point.

Here is the point. My father died when I was nine—a blow to our family of five kids. It wasn't expected and of course, it certainly wasn't welcomed. He was the ideal father, and we were a close-knit family. My mother was left to raise us all and try to make us into upstanding citizens. We weren't poor, nor were we rich. Like many others back then, my mother had to work full-time.

When I look back into those days, I realize that she carried on without missing a beat. Were things perfect? I don't know. I suppose they weren't at times, but they weren't any different than my friends' families who still had both parents and both sets of grandparents!

Why is this so important?

As I look around today, I see people with families who make every day seem like a chore. I don't have children, but I do have dogs. The issues that arise when raising dogs is often similar to the issues that occur while raising children...sometimes the similarities are uncanny. There are times when all dogs are sick, or they are mischievous, or demanding attention or they bring me to the brink of insanity. Then I think back to my mother, who at the time of my childhood, had to take care of five kids, two dogs, and her aging mother! I just do not know how she did it and did it without resorting to any vices.

I suppose this serves as a tribute to my mom who thankfully still pulls it together nicely. It is also a tribute to many of the moms (and dads) out there that are raising children on their own. I have to say it must be one of the most difficult things to raise a family, keep it together and not become a victim of your own circumstance. It's a tremendous feat to achieve what needs to be done, to put your children first and your own life second.

Not having children of my own was a choice, but if I did have them, I wouldn't even know how I'd find the time to raise them. A heartfelt kudos to those single parents and guardians who make it happen.

What is the Big Deal?

Even though I don't have children, I am well aware of what a big deal it is to raise kids as a single parent.   I remember what we expected/wanted/needed as children, and I assume not much has changed since then, aside from adding laptops, tablets and cell phones to the list of wants.

The Good, the Bad, the Ugly

I was watching "Everybody Loves Raymond" recently, and it was an episode where Ray's overbearing mother admits she read Ray's childhood diary. Do you remember that episode? She was upset because one day he had written "I hate my mom" although it was in code. She still understood it.

It made me laugh. However, it also made me realize what parents must go through each and every day. They must wonder if their kids hate them, and then they must wonder if they are doing the right thing. I know from raising dogs that it is necessary to make decisions every day. Some days it becomes such the norm that it doesn't even feel like a decision until something serious happens. That is when the self-questioning begins. "Did I do the right thing? Could I have done something differently? Are they safe? What food should they eat?"

Parents need to worry about the safety of their children. The need to concern themselves with education. Will their children need a tutor or extra help? How about life experiences or bullying? When is it time to step in? Is it necessary to keep up with the Jones's? Do the kids need to have a cell phone at age 5? What about vacations and excursions. Are they too young to watch that horror movie? Should I bring Johnny to the emergency room or try to treat it here? What if something goes wrong? Is it okay to have a babysitter? A nanny?

I am sure that this list can grow infinitely long. From what foods the children should eat to discussing life and everything in it.

When you are the decision maker, all you can do is rely on your knowledge, your experiences, and your gut instincts. You can only do the best that you can with what you have.

Since becoming an adult, I have gained a whole new respect for my mother who still answers the phone with a smile on her face and never once exclaimed "poor me" when I am sure that complaint would have been valid.

It doesn't hurt once in a while to show appreciation for those who have helped you along the way. Telling someone that they did something (or a lot of things) right might be just the thing to make their day, so it may be worth it to pick up the phone and say "Thank you!"

And Now Another Kind of Tribute...

Disclaimer: This was written in good fun. My mother and I are very close, and I enjoy teasing her about somewhat peculiar ways. She has come to visit me in Las Vegas, and we always have a good time, although, there have been certain days when I'd question my sanity. Perhaps you've experienced this with your parents? What follows is a colorful description of my mom's frequent visits. Don't worry. She's read this and has given her approval. I guess because she knows it to be true. It's a tribute to her, so to speak, one that I think you'll find comical.

Do you have that person that visits? The one whom you love with all of your heart, but can make you crazy? For me, that person is my dear mother.

Since moving to Vegas, I've been afforded the wonderful opportunities of having my family visit from time to time. Mostly my mother. Her name is Jane...or more accurately, Calamity Jane.

Rest assured, I have evidence to back this up.

When I first moved to the west coast, I had just moved into a cute little house. It even still had that new house smell to it.

The rooms fit only a bed and a couple of dressers, but, it was perfect.

My mother landed and it was quite late, so we decided to postpone any sightseeing for the morning and just go to sleep early. We were to wake up early the next day. Early to the normal person is maybe 6 or 7 am, right? Just keep that in mind.

Since it was new surroundings, I offered my mother a nightlight to which she replied, "No Thanks, I have my own."

Okay, no worries there.

Not five minutes later, I hear a pop, a sizzling sound, the electric turns off, and I smell smoke.

My mother innocently comes out of her room and says her nightlight exploded. Exploded. Have you ever heard of such a thing? I go and check and sure enough, in the dark of night, I could barely make out the broken fragments of glass on the floor from the bulb.

Doing my best to keep the dogs away, we go and reset the circuit breakers. Lights are on.

Slightly annoyed, a little confused, I once again say goodnight to my mother and drift into a peaceful slumber. It's now close to midnight.

Four Hours Later

I wake to the screams of a siren that I've never heard before. Totally in a combined state of sleepiness and adrenalin, I first look at my alarm clock, thinking maybe I bought some heavy duty, industrial strength alarm that was used to wake dinosaurs. When I realized it wasn't that, my second thought was that the house was burning down.

Looking for the light switch, I found I didn't need one as there was a bright glow coming from the downstairs. Possibly someone broke in! That's what the alarm was!

Oh wait, that might've made sense except we didn't have a burglar alarm installed yet.

No, not a burglar alarm at all.

There in the kitchen was my mother fully dressed, holding a butter knife in one hand and a piece of toast in the other. At 4 AM.

By the time I got my heart beating to a normal rhythm, my dogs to stop barking and the alarm to shut off, it was probably more like 5 AM. Too early to get up but too late to go back to sleep.

Luckily, the rest of that trip went smoothly, and I thought maybe her next visit would be a little more like easy street.

I was wrong.

I've often wondered why I can sometimes get anxious, attributing it to factors at work or perhaps the stress associated with rescuing an adult or ailing dog.

But, I think I've figured out the root. I'm pretty sure this is it.

Realizing that my wonderful mother requires a scheduled list of events when she visits, I created one, partially to placate her, partly to keep us from gambling our wages away for a relatively inexpensive price; that is if you think a price tag can be applied to sanity.

We decided to go to an exercise class. This went off without a hitch. Easy peasy.

Then there was the museum. Just a walk about museum outdoors with different landmarks and older refurbished homes. More of a simulated walk through history, including old bus depots, printing presses, general stores.

The perfect photo op.

That is, if you know how to use your camera.

As we're walking through, every couple of steps, I hear my mother complaining. "I don't know why I can't see through the viewfinder."

Me: "Let me see, Mom. Hmm-not sure, but let's use my camera and I'll give you copies of the pictures."

Mom: "Okay."

Two seconds pass.

"I just don't know why I can't see through it."

Me: "Sigh. I don't know, Ma. I can't figure it out. Let's use mine. We'll figure it out later."

We walk a few more steps.

Mom: "Oh dammit!"

Me: "What?" I turn around as we are walking through this outdoor museum to see my mother in disarray. The string for her eyeglasses which were dangling around her neck got caught on the strap for the camera, which was also dangling loosely around her neck.

She is peering down at her glasses, fumbling with strings that are only making her quandary that much worse. A look of annoyance aimed at me. Like I am the one who wrapped both cords around each other.

Her reply, in her less than cordial tone, again more of a yell. "I'm stuck. This damn camera!"

Of course, I go to help her. She is my mother, after all. Once we become untangled, I take a deep breath and break down into a nervous fit of laughter. We trudge on.

Learning to ignore my mother's continuous complaints about not being able to see through her camera's viewfinder, we walk. I try to distract her from her camera, but the complaints snowball. I urge her to use mine, to which, for reasons I simply don't understand, she holds by the center of her torso to aim a picture at me. At this point, I cry and vow to drink heavily that evening, but...I'm driving. No drinks for me.

The Next Day:

I wake up to feed the dogs and try to run back to my bedroom to fall back asleep before my mother comes out of hers at 5 am, because I know she'll try to carry on a full conversation, probably have her date book with her and try to plan the next ten years of my life.

The previous morning she caught me stumbling toward the dog's feeding bowl, eyes closed, hair disheveled, clear to anyone human that I didn't sleep and she has the audacity to ask me "Did you sleep well?"

I make it to my room, somewhat winded, but I fall back asleep, dogs in tow.

Once I wake up and shower, we head to photography class. I planned this because she's been saying how she's wanted to go to one for the past two years. I realize she is spending three hours in unknown territory, can't see through her viewfinder, so I pray. I pray and pray some more.

But, we arrive and apparently I didn't pray loud enough. We walk into a warehouse; that is dark, cold, dingy, messy, unorganized with hard wooden chairs to sit on.

My heart starts to flutter. I shake my head, close my eyes and pray before I turn to see my mother's expression.

Oh no.   Just as I thought. Although my mother doesn't curse, it's more or less the look of "Are you ^#($#&   kidding me?"

Before she even complains, I mutter, "Let's just see how it is."

Of course, that opens the door for her to complain about her viewfinder in her camera. I pray for the class to be canceled, but no such luck.

The class starts and my mother is whispering little words of aggravation with me. In a sing-song, but in no way loving tone-does she say to me, " I should've gone to the casino." Singing this mind you. I try to ignore her.

"I can't see through my viewfinder." Still freaking singing. Me, about to lose my mind, say that maybe the instructor can help her.

Listen everyone, I know that he can't.

I know there's no way in hell he can help. But it buys me time. Perhaps a kidnapper will take me away. No such luck.

The class continues. I see my mother next to me, falling asleep. We're very visible in the second row. I nudge her just in time. She jolts herself awake and looks at the instructor as if she's been drugged. That's fine. At least, she's not complaining.

Until the first hour passes.

It's a three-hour class.

Oh no, she just turned toward the person next to her. She whispers something. I see her pointing to her camera. Oh no. The viewfinder. She's telling the person next to her. I'm sweating. It's freezing, but I'm sweating. She's getting louder, and my pulse is racing.

Finally, we break because it's time to take pictures. She sees the instructor. I remember my suggestion that he may be able to help. He's obviously busy, setting things up, carrying heavy lighting equipment, but no, she chases him. "Excuse me! Excuse me!" Her voice is the only thing I heard. He looks at her, "One minute ma'am."

She's concerned again.

He comes back. She asks. He responds. He can't help. She says aloud, "He can't help." I'm scared. I don't know where she's going with this, but, it's her turn to shoot pictures of the models. She gets a picture. Now, by this time, the entire class knows she can't see out of her camera, but she got a damn picture.

Now she's at least having fun.

We leave. I'm starving and suggest the Italian restaurant by my house.

We go. We order. My meal comes. Let me reiterate. It was MY meal. It's penne a la vodka, except it is in a cereal bowl with about ten pieces of pasta. No real exaggeration there. There truly was about ten pieces.

We start heading home. I'm starving. But yet, somehow, this

minute bowl of pasta affects her more intensely.

"I can't believe they gave you a cereal bowl."

"I know, Mom."

"I mean, who do they think they are?"

"I don't know Mom. Let's just go home. It's fine."

"How do they expect to do any business? A cereal bowl? They didn't even give us any bread." Now, she's right there. Any fine Italian restaurant will give bread.

"I, I just don't know, Mom. It's fine really. I'm fine."

I'm ripping my hair out of my head, rocking back and forth, speaking in tongues, hoping for it to stop. I finally understand how crazy people go crazy. Get ready, here it is...

They know my mom. It doesn't matter how they met her or how insignificant the meeting might've seemed.

They. Know. My. Mom.

They started off sane, and slowly, carefully, strategically, she stripped away every piece of their mind.

She calls fifteen people and tells them about the subpar dining experience.

My doorbell rings. I think for sure it's the news station, but no, it's just my neighbor. I urge her to leave, quietly and quickly, pointing the way out. She heeds my advice.

I feel good knowing I saved, at least, one life.

We get ready to go to a show. I'm starving. I don't want to tell her because I know she'll start up again, but I have to eat something.

I cringe as I make my food. "If they would've given you a meal, you wouldn't be hungry right now. I mean, thankfully, you got the salad."

"Yeah mom, the salad helped. It's fine. I'll just make an English muffin. I'm fine."

We go to the show. I think it's over, but no, no, it's not over. Not at all.

The show starts and the music's blasting. I feel her eyes on me.

Her stare penetrates my soul like tiny daggers. I try to ignore it.

I never dance in public, but I start moving in my seat, snapping my fingers, swinging my hair, looking for a moshing pit.

There is none; it's a Frank Sinatra/Dean Martin imitation. I dance like there's no tomorrow, hoping she'll stop looking at me.

I have to give in.

They say anticipation of a bad situation is worse than the actual situation itself.

In comparison, the penetration of her stare is more potent than the music itself.

I brace myself and slowly turn toward her.

She's mouthing something. The music is still blasting. I'm waiting for whatever bout of craziness she's about to bestow upon me.

"Yeah, Mom?"

"Did you have to pay extra for
that salad?"

~The End~

I'm fortunate to have a mother who
will laugh at my version, (even
though, I will admit) it is slightly
exaggerated. Trust me, she has seen
this and has written her own version
in retaliation!

Lesson 17-Go Ahead. Go For a Swim!

I remember one year, when winter had made its blistery appearance throughout the nation, we mostly heard of bursts of frigid weather accompanied by dozens of inches of snowfall.

One of the advantages of moving out west to Las Vegas is that while we endure some cold weather, and it snows in the mountain regions, the valley is, for the most part, dry and warmer. The tradeoff, of course, is temperatures that soar above 115 in the midst of the summer. The climate becomes so warm that our cars need dashboard covers, steering wheel covers and we need to exercise caution when putting on our seat belts to avoid getting burned by the metal.

Since we hadn't joined in with the rest of the nation's inclement weather, the sun still shone in Vegas, but temperatures had not yet become acceptable to warrant swimming.

That is unless you were a golden retriever.

At the time, there were three retrievers in the house. One of them was a Nova Scotia Duck Tolling Retriever.

Retrievers are known for their love of water, but only one of ours fit that stereotype, and it was our female golden retriever. If you've ever seen her picture before, chances are she was dripping wet in it.

Toffee, the duck toller, had no interest and Duke, our male golden retriever found enjoyment in wading, but wouldn't venture any further than that. If we swam during the summer, he might have punched the water and expressed interest, but he hadn't found the nerve. He was curious, as he always gazed at Brandi in wonder whenever she took a dip.

One November when Brandi had swum, she exited the pool shivering, with her teeth chattering. After drying her off and warming her up, I forbade her to go in for the rest of the winter. She begrudgingly obliged, although she still made attempts. I had one saving grace because Brandi used to look back at me before she took a dip and waited for me to say "okay." If I didn't say it, she wouldn't swim.

Over the winter, her age had begun to show a bit, and while she was never overexcited, she had slowed down. She was approaching the ripe old age of thirteen, and I didn't expect her to run marathons.

It had been mid-February, and it was nearly seventy degrees. As she went outside, she gave me the look, and I wasn't sure if I should say "okay." The weather was warm enough for her to dry off quickly, so I wasn't worried about her being too cold this time. I was worried, however, that since she was a bit older, she wouldn't be able to swim quite right.

However, I wanted her to be happy, so I went outside with her, stood by the pool ready to jump into the freezing water if I had to help her, and gave her the green light.

It had been a few months, so she had been a little rusty, but she slowly eased in and found her bearings. Her first lap made me inch closer, as she didn't look so sure of herself. By the second lap, she had found her mojo. She was back.

Since that day, she had gone in a few times and swam like a champ.

Confident and graceful, her tail was wagging. I had no doubt there was a smile on her face.

Once she was in, she tested the waters so to speak, and when I called her to exit the pool, she did one more lap before obeying my command. No, never once did I get mad at her. I knew she loved it, but I didn't want her to get too tired.

It is one of those memories that I cherish and one that taught me well. Even though I couldn't fathom going swimming in February, I would have risked everything if Brandi had even needed my assistance.

Seeing her happy was more important than my own happiness (or warmth) at that moment.

Sometimes in life, it's necessary to take a swim. In other words, put the happiness of others before your own and do whatever it takes to see them smile. It might be a smile that you remember for years to come.

Brandi is no longer with us, but the videos of her "smiling" as she swam are something that I often watch, and is a confirmation that she was, indeed, happy.

So, go ahead. Now and then go for a swim in life. If not for yourself, then to make someone else happy if only for a little while.

Lesson 18-Enjoy Life!

Enjoy Life. Oh, we've seen our dogs doing this, haven't we? Simple things such as tossing a tennis ball in the air and catching it, to running in the park, to simply throwing themselves on the ground in the freezing snow to wiggle around and make the doggy version of snow angels.

Dogs make it appear effortless to enjoy life. They don't have complex conversations or debates. They don't ever ask for much, aside from a cuddle, some treats and perhaps a walk once in a while.

Their cheerfulness usually comes easy when they have families that love them. They don't think negatively. They just have fun and enjoy life!

People have it a little tougher, although it doesn't always need to be difficult. While many of us try to incorporate positive thoughts into our daily routine, some days present more obstacles than others. That giant beast of negativity tries its hardest to creep into the corners of our sponge-like minds and set up his dominoes so that that one negative thought leads surreptitiously into another.

If we're not careful, before long those positive thoughts are a thing of the past, and we only see the ominous cloud of doom eternally lingering over our heads.

What we fail to realize is that one bad day doesn't equal a lifetime of disappointment. Though we may struggle to shed the bad times, we need to remember that good times do exist ahead. It won't always be easy; though we'd like it to be. Sometimes clouds don't necessarily mean there is sadness ahead. Sometimes they signify an uplifting change.

When I began writing and self-publishing my books, I went through a plethora of emotions; some good, some bad, some of elation, uncertainty, hope, or despair.

I didn't know what I was doing, nor did I know what to expect. It was a big step. It was something I had always wanted to do and didn't know anyone who had done it. I had no one to ask for advice. It was truly the first time I was really in it alone. A magnificent but terrifying experience, as I'd imagine any big step would be.

In my first book, Finally Home, I preceded each chapter with a quote, never realizing the feedback I'd receive on those quotes. My readers told me they loved them. And so did I.

As a matter of fact, I loved them so much that I designed another book—this time on quotes— called

Bark Out Loud. If you've read my bio or my previous books, it's no secret about how I feel about animals...and it's also reflected in this book.

What I didn't reveal in the book is explanations to any of those quotes, and some (if not all) I feel deserve some further detail. I've included only a handful of them here for you, just in case you're having one of those blah days, just reminding you to enjoy life. Hopefully, these might put things in perspective.

Without further ado...

Just noticing the simplicity of my dogs' happiness is enough to make me realize that it is often the little things in life that are most important.

And it truly is the little things in life. During the hustle and bustle of a crazy work week or whatever you have that is piled high on your plate, it's easy to lose sight that it is often the simplest of things that provide the greatest enlightenment and joy.

Nothing brightens up the day like a big smile from your pups upon entering the room!

For me, it is my pup's smile, but it can be the smile from your child or grandchild or your best friend for that matter. Do you ever notice that on a mundane Saturday afternoon, while flicking through old photographs of people or animals no longer with us, that we yearn for those "old times" when so and so was alive, the so-called happier days? Now think back a little further. During those days, did you realize you were happy or did you take it for granted? If you realized it, then kudos to you! A lot of people don't know what they have until they no longer have it. A smile from my pup is something I won't always have, so I enjoy it in the here and now. If we could master this for everything in our life, it would enhance our happiness quotient considerably. We always long for the past or fear the future, but living in the here and now is exactly where we should be.

Being a hero to someone, even if it is a dog, is a feeling like no other. Though it can be frustrating, it can be the most rewarding thing to give someone a second chance at a happy life.

While some may classify dog rescue as a selfless act, it truly goes both ways. Yes, you are saving a dog's life, but in many cases, they are saving yours as well. Sometimes you don't even realize it in the beginning. I wrote Paw Prints in the Sand: Mission Accomplished with this exact moral in mind. There is something to be said for the unconditional love we receive from our pets. And often, they are bringing enjoyment to our life as well.

There are too many dogs roaming free out there, partly due to negligence on the part of the owners. Unfortunately, there are only so many dogs that can be saved. Dogs cannot speak, so, when possible, it is up to us to verbalize for them.

The only thing wrong with trying to please everyone is that there's always, at least, one person who will remain unhappy. You.

If I can get one point across, it's this one. I've given up trying to be a people pleaser. It's impossible. Critics are everywhere, and everyone can do it better, no matter what "it" is. I've observed and listened to friends, co-workers, acquaintances who have the biggest hearts yet beat themselves up because this one wasn't happy or that one wasn't happy...even though they gave everything they had. Not everyone will always be happy, and you will drive yourself to the point of insanity if you try to please everyone. Do yourself a favor. If you can face yourself in the mirror at the end of the day, then you did okay. Don't worry about everyone else.

Remember, just because someone is smiling, it doesn't mean they aren't holding back tears.

Some people I've been fortunate to meet along my journey through life always have something nice to say even if they are in a horrible situation. They always have a smile and on the surface seem to have a wonderful   life.   In   private conversations   with   these   same people, you may find out they are in the midst of a terrible divorce, or their parent just died, or they just lost their job. Behind closed doors, tears stream down their cheeks.

My point is when people are ready to use their razor sharp tongue (and many of us are guilty of this, myself   included!),   perhaps   first realize that another person may be acting a certain way because of a private situation they are enduring. Kind words might be just what they need instead of a verbal lashing. You know what they say about catching more flies with honey.

What makes someone better than someone else? The answer? Nothing. Everyone has their own weaknesses.

We've all come across those people who resign themselves to being better than someone else. Instead of teaching, they ridicule. Instead of helping, they bully. I have the greatest respect for those who decide to teach those who might not know the answer. For those who decide to help someone get up from a fall. No one is better than anyone else. More educated? Possibly. More experienced. Definitely. But not better.

Often, the reason that you make mistakes is to learn from them and teach someone else.

Lastly, many will beat themselves up for making a mistake. They forget that they are human. Did you ever look at it this way? For every situation you failed at, use it to help someone else succeed. Life is a series of lessons. The fact that you made a mistake means that you tried. Sure, it's easy to breeze through life without making any attempt at following your dream or reaching your goal. Sure, you can then say you never made a mistake. But why? Make a mistake? Pick yourself up, brush yourself off and try again. Then look back at that mistake and yes, laugh.

My point in a nutshell? Enjoy your life. Dream big. And chase those dreams. Can't catch them? So what. You tried. Does a dog get depressed if they can't catch that squirrel? Nope! They just move on to the next one and try, try again. Life flies by in a blink. Get out there and enjoy it.

Lesson 19-On Writing

Writing is one of the topics that motivated me to bring this book to fruition, besides my love of dogs and the real-life lessons they had taught me. I wanted to discuss experiences learned during my writing career. It is, of course, one of the things I'm passionate about. The last two chapters are dedicated to just that. You'll find some tips about indie writing, pitfalls, and writer's block, along with some motivation and more. Enjoy!

Why Writing?

There's a look that is apparent in the eyes of almost every author. A need that dwells inside longing to be set free. It's determination. Perseverance. All of those power words that accompany a strong desire and a yearning to succeed. Perhaps some want to become famous, while for many, it's a personal goal for which fame doesn't play a role.

It's the passion of writing. To some, it's a craft, a hobby. To others, it's a possible opportunity to make a living.

It's an apple that hasn't yet been peeled to the core, but there are layers upon layers of self-discovery. Data and stories. Imagination and creativity that crave to be unleashed. Like a bird, it is waiting for the day to spread its wings and show the world how it can fly.

Writing is an art form. There are no two styles that are exactly alike. Each writer has a voice, and each voice delivers a message in its distinctive way. Driving points across differently than any other writer. Utilizing tone and diction, obeying the rules and breaking the rules with their personal style, their unique flair.

Their technique may appeal to the masses or capture the attention of a select few. Each author has their favorite topic, their area of expertise.

Writing is the ability to take a diminutive idea and develop it into something immense; something that the world has never seen before. The sky is the proverbial limit, the clouds providing ample cover for the unveiling of the writer's voice.

With each written word, a new message is conveyed, a new story told or a new piece of information divulged, and the author has come one step closer to fulfilling their need.

Writing is many things to many people. It's not a craft molded from a cookie cutter. Each author has their reasons, each has their wants, and each has a different story to tell.

Writing isn't just words that lie flat on a page; it's life experiences and decades of imagination dancing copiously on canvas.

Writing is a craft that knows of no bounds. The words dance on the stage in a choreographed promenade; the result of a creative and overly imaginative mind.

Where Does it Begin?

I've had people ask me when I began writing. It's a question for which I never know how to answer properly.

At about age seven or so, I can recall being tucked away in my bedroom, sitting on the top bunk, pillows propped up behind me, with a notebook and a pen in hand, creating what I thought would be an international masterpiece. I can remember the notebook, a Five-subject— complete with folders separating each one.   The folders were to separate each book I was going to write or, at least, each chapter.

The pen? A Bic Four-color pen, because it was imperative I could write the important words in a different color.   I also had my calligraphy set nearby. I used these pens to create the titles and subtitles. You have to remember, this was way before the days of computers, and back then, I didn't yet know how to use the typewriter...but I was learning.

With each story, I had the best of intentions, yet none of them came to fruition.   Distractions like video games or a new Barbie doll outfit came along, and the notebook sat on the top bunk, patiently waiting for me to finish the next paragraph.

How I wish I kept those notebooks to delve into the mind of a seven-year-old me, but they got stacked somewhere and were never seen again.

I suppose the real answer is when I began self-publishing, and that I can answer with certainty. I began writing my first non-fiction book in January of 2010 with Finally Home: Lessons on Life from a Free-Spirited Dog.

The Experience

I've written tiny blogs and small snippets here and there about what I've learned from writing and self-publishing, but I don't know if I ever truly expressed the voyage and the destination.

Writing is an interesting journey. You take what you've learned about commanding your native language. You remember the rules, the boundaries, the do's and don'ts. You add your individuality. You add your sense of humor (or lack thereof). You add your intelligence. You add your narrative. You try to compact all of these ingredients into an imaginary mixing bowl and decide on the recipe for your book.

You may or may not create a physical outline, or perhaps as you begin writing, you create a reverse outline. For me, that had worked best. Create the story first, worry about the outline later.

You then decide if you're going to break any of the rules of writing. After all, rules were meant to be broken.   You need to add your creative talent.   Without even knowing it, you develop a writing style.   When you write enough, people begin to notice and recognize your style.   They either like it, or they don't. They can either relate or think you're off of your rocker. And that, is one of the things they don't tell you about when publishing a book.

The Critics

You've written your book. Your friends and family have all told you that you were funny, or smart, or had great story-telling knack. Whatever it is that you have believed about yourself, you utilized those skills in your writing.

And then you realize the unwritten truth. Reviews are subjective. Some people get you. Others do not. This point is perhaps one of the most important things to remember, especially when you take your hard work, your imaginative panache, your personality, and you open your arms wide, expose your heart and throw all of it out there for the entire world to notice.

Of course, everyone is going to like it, right? Your friends do. Your family does. Strangers have emailed you and pressed the contact button on your website to tell you how much they like it, but there are millions upon millions of people in the world.   Here's a tip. Not all are going to "get you."

Change What's Necessary, but Not Yourself

The only thing wrong with trying to please everyone is that there's always at least one person who will remain unhappy. You.

When you get bad reviews, it's difficult to refrain from yelling and screaming, but the truth is that sometimes, there is helpful knowledge in those reviews. Granted, there are some people chock full of ill-intent whose main objective is to belittle and judge, but there are some who truly have found some issues.

A professional editor can help by finding of grammatical issues, timeline issues, or the issues that occur when you get on a hot streak and type so fast your fingers fly off of the keyboard. The moment might have been exciting for you possibly as your story gains momentum, but you might have left off an important word or two. Have your editor FIND those errors!

Those are the easy critiques. Then, some may not like your story, your style, your humor. All I can say is that everyone is different. I had a conversation with friends about books one day. In a group of five, each had their opinion about what was considered decent writing and what some considered boring. We discussed authors like Stephen King and Dean Koontz. I like them both, but love Koontz for a few reasons. One, he has an insane sense of humor. I love it. Two, he loves golden retrievers (enough said there) and three, his vocabulary is so advanced that I learn new words when reading his books.

What don't I like? A lot of detail. What do my friends love? TONS of detail! Right there, we would offer two distinctly different reviews on a book based on the amount of detail alone.

Some like dark stories. Some like humor.

Now, regarding humor. I'm rarely serious. Needless to say, in a public setting, many of my off-the-wall conversations are lost on those who are eternally serious. While I can have some people in stitches, with others, I get a blank stare. I'd imagine those who stare at me blankly would have no interest in my books. And that's okay. The bottom line? You can't appeal to everyone.

I've also had conversations with people about certain comedians that I find hilarious. I understand the sarcasm and quick wit, while others have claimed, they found them to be boring. Two different opinions, but is one better than the other? Nope. Just different.

It's the same with writing. Some people will "get you." Others never will. You cannot and never will be able to please everyone. It's virtually impossible.

Improve your craft as best as you can. Read more and write more. Learn more.

But don't change yourself.

Since I've begun on my writing journey, I've come across a multitude of experiences that you can't learn about in a "Do-It-Yourself" manual. At least, none that I have read.

Some I can easily label as rewarding, such as my first good review. To be blatantly honest, I didn't even realize that reviews were possible on Amazon. I come from the world where you see a book in a bookstore; it sounds interesting, you buy it, and you take your chances. If you didn't like it, you gave it away. But reviews which are now so common, were an entirely new feature to me. I couldn't help but feel overjoyed that someone took the time to review MY book!

Then, my first bad review. That wasn't fun at all.

These days, if you've done anything publicly from forming a business, to creating an indie movie, to making a sale or a buy on eBay or you have written a book, there is a good chance that someone, somewhere is going to give you a review. Welcome to the age of technology!

In comparison with about twenty years ago when the Internet was only taking baby steps toward its popularity, more data is now readily available to the public. Is this what we want? Well, there are two ways to look at that.

I had to accept that I was going to get reviews. Some good and some not so good. Traditionally published books also get good and bad reviews. No one is exempt!

The good ones are phenomenal. The fact that my comical books about dogs have made someone chuckle or have inspired someone to adopt a dog is enough of a high to make my day. It's also a learning experience of what type of people are reading my books and discover their sense of humor. Reviews are also a fascinating gauge to determine if readers enjoyed reading the sections of the book that I found the funniest while I was writing it.

That same theory is applicable as it pertains to my thrillers. The purpose of a psychological thriller, in my mind, is to is to cause the reader to be a bit on edge, provide drama and a healthy dose of jittery horror. So, when readers review and say they were spooked a little or a lot, and they were at least mildly entertained, then it was all worth it.

The bad reviews are not all necessarily bad. You may read this and exclaim WHAT?? Let me explain.

Of course, when reviews are written with pure hatred, you begin to wonder if the reviewer knows you personally. "Hmm- did I cut them off on the freeway?" "Did we fight on the playground when we were younger?"

But, when the honest ones point out errors the writer might not have realized, or give an alternate perspective, they can be helpful. If they didn't care for your style of writing, it just goes to prove the adage that everyone has different tastes, and you can't please everyone. As many indie writers will tell you, the unfortunate part of what we do is that we can't fit editing into the budget, at least not at first.

So, we are left with no other options but to read our stories over and over and over again, obsessing over paragraphs and refining them until our eyes can no longer see straight. We try to go to unbiased acquaintances to read our stories as well, to capture errors we may have overlooked. As far as content is concerned, well, that is all the writer's individual style. It appeals to some and not to others.

With Finally Home, I've received emails from readers saying it was one of the funniest books they've read. Then, I've seen reviews that say otherwise.

There is one issue with reviews. Reviews are like having an argument for which tape is stuck to your lips and you can't defend yourself. You can't voice your opinion or explain yourself.

With Finally Home, someone had emailed me to voice their opinion about me buying Brandi from a pet store. I'll clarify that it is true and yes, while puppy mills may have existed many years ago, I was not informed as I am now about them.

Facebook didn't exist, and the Internet was only in its beginning stages. Puppy mills weren't discussed often, so I didn't know of the horror. I had no clue.

But, I don't regret our decision to buy Brandi for one moment, as I found one of the loves of my life in that store. Since then, I only adopt dogs, donate as much as I can toward their rescue, volunteer for rescue groups when time permits, and will never buy another dog. I've written a book series ON puppy mills, called Paw Prints in the Sand, trying to raise awareness the best that I can. But, I digress.

I've made it a point to read books by indie authors, (especially when they run free promotions) and give them an honest review. If I find that there are errors or inconsistencies, I email the author so that they can fix them up. After all, we're all in this together.

Pitfalls and Things to Look For

When I begin writing a new book, I have it all mapped out in my mind. The basis for the plot, the characters, the scenery. It usually starts off slowly and then, like a snowball, it gains consistent momentum. There are times when the day has turned to night, and chapters will get written before I realize my fingers are cramped, and I need to take a break. What happens? The story came alive.

By the time I complete my book, it might be months before I've reread the first chapter. It's at that moment that I realize some things need to change. I go back first and check for edits. Yes, even though I send it off to an editor, I go through numerous times to find any error and believe me, there are always edits. Then, I go back again and look for inconsistencies. Did someone have blond hair, blue eyes in one scene and brown eyes in another? It happens!

Then, I go back again. Are the timelines accurate? Is it Spring, Summer or Fall? Did they just go to the beach and then go skiing in the next chapter?

Once I address all of these important tidbits, I read it once more. I don't believe in fluffing up a story just to add pages, but I do believe in adding enough description so that the reader is there with you, spicing up their imagination and enjoying the journey. I don't want them to stumble over words or have to read a sentence twice.

After about the fifth or sixth read, I create a title, send to an editor and while I'm waiting for my manuscript back full of red lines, I design my cover and with any luck, my trailer.

It's a long expedition, but one that is well worth it. There is always room to improve and always techniques to learn. One of the most practical methods that I found to improve my writing was to increase my reading. I'll always have my style, but there are unlimited ways to progress upon that style and add more finesse.

One thing was constant; I had always written something. I didn't always necessarily write a novel. In fact, it could've been anything. Sometimes, I'd just scribble my name, other times a paragraph that went nowhere. On a rainy day, when I was stuck indoors, I'd fill up a document with a short tale.

When people ask me how do I motivate myself to write, sometimes it's just as easy as sitting down in a chair, now with my laptop instead of a pen and paper, (although I still have a fascination with pens and notepads)!

You've probably heard of free-association writing before. If not, it's a technique that was developed many years ago by Sigmund Freud and his co-worker, and is used to explore your subconscious mind and simply write. It's a fascinating theory because it does put your conscious mind to rest and allow you to type (or handwrite); whatever comes easily or more naturally to you. There have been moments when I've practiced this and have fabricated a storyline that I love; while other times what I see on the screen in front of me is just a "download" of what's been floating around in my mind.

I bring this up because it's a conducive exercise to perform before sitting down to write a manuscript. It takes the pressure off having to "make sense" and puts the mind in a relaxed state.

Writing doesn't always have to be what you want the public to see. While I don't have a physical journal, often I will take ten minutes out of my day to type one up in a Word document and delete it all once I'm satisfied that my mind is free of tension and clear enough to begin writing an actual book.

In one of my psychological thrillers called "Phobia," the protagonist, Matt's entire life was recorded in a journal that he had written in daily. At first, I wasn't sure if men kept journals, but I asked around, and some did admit to me that they did! Some used a physical notebook, but others went the most traditional route and typed up their deepest thoughts in a password protected Word document or online source. Although, after what happens to Matt in Phobia, some may think twice about having the possibility of their private thoughts available to anyone!

I became especially enthusiastic about writing when I penned Phobia.

It was a pleasurable book to write. Yes, I know. It's a thriller. It shouldn't have been pleasurable! But, I loved the characters that I created, either for their genuine congeniality or their extremely evil tendencies. I can't speak for other authors, but I develop a complete visual of my characters. I envision how they speak, whether they have a twang or an accent, what they look like and I "get into their heads" to give them their own personality. I would imagine other authors would have to do this to make each character inimitable.

Writing thrillers is much different than writing dog-related books, as you can imagine. To write a thriller, you have to tap into a compartmentalized section of your mind and apply some twisted plots!

There had been times when I have even scared myself and removed some scenes from the story. Believe me when I say that when you're the one writing a story, it is still very easy to get spooked, especially if writing while no one is home on a dark stormy night. There have been times I had to put the computer away and stop because I scared myself too much! I had been writing Evil's Door, and the visual in my mind got way too real!

Some people have asked me where I get my ideas from to write thrillers. I've been watching thrillers and reading scary stories ever since I can remember. I also read a lot of true crime books. While what I read and watch does still frighten me, I find that I am intrigued. My imagination takes over and turns ordinary every day, non-scary situations and embellishes them into a full-blown thriller.

Also, a lot of the material from my books originate from dreams (or nightmares) that I have. I've been keeping a dream log for years, as I'm one of those people who remember almost every dream. With one of my books, Unwanted Dreams, the bulk of this book is put together from recurring nightmares. It was the first thriller I've ever written, but I still love to reread it now and again. It is still my favorite. The story taps into every emotion and leaves the reader pondering the story way after they are done reading it.

The ideas for my dog-related books come a bit easier. I've never been without a dog in my life, so I've watched their behavior, observed their body language and witnessed all different types of scenarios of owners with their dogs. Writing a book about dogs is really about taking normal life experiences and giving them a bit of a twist. Many of my dog books are Non-Fiction, so they border on the line of biography as well.

Indie Writing

These days so many authors are taking the route of self-publishing, otherwise known as Independent Writing or Indie Writing. While independent publishing involves more work than getting a traditional publisher, I love that it gives me the opportunity to take creativity to the next level. The writing is mine, the covers are created by me and the marketing and advertising are all done to my liking. It's a full-time job crammed into a part-time schedule, but it's worth it in the end. It's fun and gives me an opportunity to donate to animal rescue.

I hate to admit it, but for a while, I was one of those closed-minded people. When I saw an indie album or indie movie without any legendary stars, I'd roll my eyes and skip to the next blockbuster film.

I didn't even know that indie books existed up until a few years ago, as they weren't as popular.

Wow, how the past few years have changed my views.

I've since given indie music and movies a try as well. Many of them have left me walking away with a new perspective. Some of the musicians or actors —who are not famous— DO have talent.

Now that I've traveled down the path of Indie Author Road, I've become a little more sensitive to grammatical and spelling errors in traditionally published books, as well as my own. I won't go as far to say that I no longer make mistakes, because I do, but I'm now more aware of catching errors when I read any book.

One of the most difficult things about writing a book—in my mind—is not coming up with the material for stories. I have zillions of ideas. It's not writer's block. It's

not even the formatting, the
marketing, the creation of book
trailers, websites or social media. It
is the editing. Editing is difficult
which is why I preach that whenever
possible, a professional editor is the
way to go.

**You've Finished Writing. Now,
What?**

Congratulations. Whew. That
was tough. But it gets tougher. You
are an indie writer, remember? The
unpaved road, the obstacles, the
inclement weather...remember all
that?

You are ready to get started on
the rest of your journey. Be aware,
there might be some roadblocks.

Overcoming Writer's Block

As a writer, I often wonder what strategies other authors utilize when they encounter a debilitating case of writer's block. I haven't come across it too often, but when I do, here's a few pointers that usually help. These not only alleviate writer's block but are often refreshing ways to help solve other mind-benders as well!

1. Stop writing. What?! Yep. Stop writing. It may take only an hour, or it may take a week. Heck, it may even take a month! Sometimes the pressure one puts on themselves to complete a task causes more harm than good. Taking a break, revitalizing the mind often kicks things into perspective. It might even cause an electrifying surge of ideas. Be ready to have your pen handy when it does!

2. Explore somewhere different. We have tendencies to follow the same humdrum routine every day. You may just be tired and bored of staring at the same monotonous scenery day in and day out. It doesn't have to a worldwide vacation, but just somewhere out of

the norm. Take a ride down a street you've never driven. Take a different route to work. Sometimes I trek out into the desert. I never know what kind of inspiration I'll find there. Or the beach. Or sitting atop a quiet mountain. A transcending perspective often inspires beguiling ideas.

3. People watch(or, dog watch)! Where? Anywhere! At the gas station, at an airport, on an airplane, in the mall. Wherever! It can help you awaken your imagination and gather ideas for the description of your characters.

4. Writing a Comedy? Watch something funny. Writing a thriller? Flirt with your fears and get Scared! For "Phobia," I thought of any fear I had possessed and any fears that

frightened other people and thought of the worst possible thing that could happen—you tell your fears to a homicidal maniac. Hence, Phobia was born!

5.   Brainstorm about what you LOVE! Change genres. My first book, "Finally Home" was one of the most pleasurable books I could write. And who knew more about Buddy than me? Most people know or come to realize that I adore dogs. So I rarely run out of ideas when I write about them.

6.   Recollect   conversations you've had in the past. Remember how the conversations flowed. Did one of the participants interrupt the other? How about emotions? What were you feeling at the time? What did you do with your hands? Were

they in your pocket or do you speak with your hands as well? Try to incorporate those types of ideas into your book.

7. Start Writing a Different Book. Sound crazy? Trust me, it helps! You don't have to finish the second one...or, you don't have to finish even the first. Or, you can finish both. Eventually! I've started a second book and had two books going at once. I'd write in one when I manufactured an idea, and sometimes it would be an entire month before I would write in the other. It's like having two separate journals. Of course, each time I let a month lapse, I'd have to reread what I had written, but it truly helped me stay on course.

8.   Surf the web.   Rummage through old photo albums.   Seeing photos of interesting people or things or reminiscing over old photos   could   spark   your imagination.   You may find that images of old furniture or clothing from the 70's give you enough dazzling material for an entire chapter!

9. Exercise. An invigorating run on the treadmill, listening to high-energy music gives some quality alone time with your thoughts. You'd be surprised to discover how the mind-body connection will assist in sketching new material!

Not feeling motivated? Get out there and go for a walk. Something will inspire you...

Elizabeth Parker Books

10. Sleep. If you don't dream much, this may not help you. But, for someone like me who has vivid dreams constantly, sleep is one of my best tools. I had awakened with an entire storyline for "Unwanted Dreams." Of course, by the time I started writing it, I'd changed a few things, but most of the material evolved from actual dreams (or nightmares)! You may even want to keep a journal by your bedside to write some ideas when you first wake up!

What to Do When Your Own Characters Appear in Your Life

I unleashed my first thriller. That was fun. I still love the book. It is called Unwanted Dreams. I took every demented thought I had, every recent scary dream and jotted it down on paper and transformed it into a book.

The only person who'd read it was my friend. I hadn't even published it yet.

About a day after my friend read it, I received an email. The email was nothing horrible, but it was from a person just giving me some advice on my website. Telling me some things that I should change. Some light critiquing. I thought it interesting, and then I saw the signature.

At first, it frightened me. It was the same name as the killer in my book. The same book that I hadn't yet published. Then, I realized, it must be my friend, of course. So, I did what any normal person would do. I called her. "Pretty funny- you had me scared there for a second."

Her response was "I'm not sure what you are talking about." After going back and forth for a few minutes, I realized…that email didn't come from her. So there I was staring at a computer screen, looking at an email signed by the namesake of the murderer in my book.

Want to talk about paranoid? How could this person email me the DAY after my friend read the book and have the same exact first and last name as the killer? I believe in coincidences, but this was too much.

A few days went by, and I visited a forum for authors where we only know each other by our ID, but not our real name.   One of them innocently asked me to critique their website. "Sure. Why not?"

The previous incident was still buried in my brain, but I was trying to forget about it.

Wouldn't you know it, after digging around, I found out the person who had written me that email was that *same* person that asked me to critique *their* website? I simply never knew his real name until I clicked on the link and voila! Mystery solved. I no longer had to question the integrity of my antivirus software, look for bugs, spyware or tracking devices!

It did give me an idea for a thriller, though, although, I haven't started writing that one yet! What interesting experiences have you come across as a write or just life in general that made you shudder just a little?

So you see? These are the lessons that you can't find in a manual, but I hope that have provided you with some knowledge...or at least a laugh or two!

Lesson 20-It's Not Always About the Money

When writing fiction of any kind, you don't just think like a writer, you become an actor. In a mere second, your voice changes to become that of your character. Your diction changes. Your accent changes. You see seasons that have long past or a dark, dismal road that has never been traveled upon.

It is the creative license that keeps an author coming back for more.

Elizabeth Parker
www.elizabethparkerbooks.com

Sadly, most of us have been living under the pretense that if you can't make money while performing a certain task, then it's not worth it.

Only later in life did I realize that while money is essential, so is enjoying life.

A few years ago, after Buddy Senior had lost his battle to cancer, I began making jewelry—mostly bracelets—and thought about an idea to personalize them for people who had lost their dogs, or who love dogs. It was all in the name of canine cancer.

The bracelets were adorable, fashioned with carefully selected beads and dog related charms, such as little dog bones, doghouses, dogs, etc. For a while, I was selling them, but because having an online store can be quite a bit of effort, I closed it down. I did, however, continue making them for friends and friends of friends, simply because I enjoyed it. The bracelets were appealing, held special meaning to me and that was reason enough.

It wasn't about the money. It was about keeping Buddy's memory and the awareness about canine cancer alive.

Then, of course, there's writing.

Writing. The Greatest Get Rich Quick scheme?

Many people have a vision about writers as though they are living the life of luxury sitting in a plush comfy chair watching the royalties roll in. I wish I could say that is true, but sadly, it is a far-fetched fantasy.

Where's the Dough?

Whether you are new to the world of writing, or if this has been your ultimate dream since you were able to pick up a pen and draw anything resembling a word, you are in for a universe of diversity.

It took a long time to reward myself with the title of "author," as in the beginning I felt like I was in some obscure club for which I had to pass the initiation phase and in a way, I was. We all are.

I happen to be an indie writer at the moment, and while I won't say whether that will change or not in the future, for now, that is the path I have chosen and have learned the ins and outs fairly well.

For those who have traversed along this bumpy road alongside me, you are most likely familiar with the tumultuous terrain, the unpredictable weather and even some of the critters that buzz from the brush. Each day varies greatly from the next, with ideas, with creativity and yes, with money.

If you learn one thing about writing, it's that it is not always about the money. If that is the only reason that some pick up a pen, then they might want to put it back down. While there is money available in writing, if you are an indie author, it will not happen overnight unless one has a magnificent budget to place on advertising.

For the masses, it is going to take time and patience for it to become a lucrative profession. It is going to require perseverance, commitment, loyalty, and dedication.

If you're an indie, you are going to need a thick skin. There are going to be critics. People who want to tear you apart, make you quit and curse your success. These people do exist, and they are just waiting on the sidelines.

Writing is a hybrid of complete jubilation and victory mixed with uncertainty and frustration. There are moments when you are on the pinnacle of a mountain and moments when you feel like crawling under a blanket and remaining there.

The common misconception that you are living a life of leisure because you have days off or nights off or (gasp) write full time is just that...a misconception.

Don't be surprised if your friends and family think that you are free to mingle or lend a hand with something because "all" you are doing is writing.

If I could offer one word of advice, make it very clear from the beginning that you are serious about it. That it isn't just a hobby. That it IS your job, whether it is full-time, part-time or only a few hours a week whenever time permits.

If you are serious about writing, (or anything in life), then you have to show it. Take yourself seriously, and everyone else will too.

My second piece of advice? Don't underestimate your work or your knowledge. While at first you will still be learning the ropes, every piece of information you acquire is, indeed, valuable. Only give your work away if you WANT to give it away.

Offering advice is fine, but you are under no obligation to be a daily coach unless you want to. What you will soon learn is that writing is not an eight-hour job, but more like a twelve to fourteen-hour job (and then some) if you consider how many hours you spend thinking about what type of book you wish to produce!

Writing Advice

One of the reasons I am writing this, and I am not a writing coach of any kind, but I do have some people who have asked for advice from time to time. I don't know everything. I don't think that anyone does. What I do know, however, I am delighted to share, and here is as good a place as any.

After trial and error, I think I have made enough mistakes for everyone!

First and foremost: A writing device is necessary. A pen and paper, a smartphone, a tablet or a laptop. Sometimes all of the above are needed. You never know when an idea is going to strike. Find which one works for you and carry it with you at all times.

Second: A camera. Now, depending on what your plans are, you might want to get a decent one. I use a camera for a couple of reasons. One, to capture scenes or characters that I want to incorporate into my book. Two, I create my book covers. One thing I learned is that your book cover should have a high resolution, quality picture. It will be the first impression that your readers will have of your work.

Your cover, per se, is your packaging. And we all know how important packaging is.

Three: An eager attitude and the ability to take constructive criticism from friends and family or a writing group. Then, the ability to take not-so-constructive criticism from readers. Both are essential, and both are not effortless!

Fourth: An idea.

Once you have all of those elements together in a nice, compact part of your studio, you are ready to begin!

One bit of advice that I had read time and time again but chose to ignore was never publish your first piece of work. I had published mine and am happy that I did so, but note that I did have to go back and edit it a few times. Save yourself the trouble and if you are going to submit your first manuscript to publish, make sure you have someone else edit it!

Now, the Writing

Once you have your general idea, there are a few ways to get started. Some people love outlines. Some people love to write summaries first. Others find it easier to store the idea in their minds, write it and then write a reverse outline to keep track as they go. I happen to enjoy the latter.

Since many of my ideas for novels have been cultivating in my mind for the past few years, I already know what I want to write, so a reverse outline works best especially when I want to change things up a little from the initial plan.

Once you decide which format you want to use, here is the moment you have been anticipating. Write! Begin your stories. End chapters with a cliffhanger. Make the reader want to go on. Make them want to read until their eyes close and the book lands on their lap or the Kindle shuts itself off.

One gotcha here. Well, two. One, don't write until YOUR eyes start to close. You are bound to make mistakes and even take the story on an unintended journey. Two, you may write an entire paragraph or heck, even an entire chapter that while at first, it sounded good, but on second glance, not so good. Don't be afraid to delete it. If you don't like it, neither will your readers. Or, you may like it but just not for your current book. Cut it out and paste it in a separate document. That paragraph may find a cozy home nestled between the pages of another book you decide to write!

Exploring Different Genres

What started off as a small dream from when I was a young kid, barely knowing how to write, with a limited selection of pens and paper, became a wonderful reality as an adult approaching my late thirties, with a collection of pens and a drawer full of notepads.

With nothing but a world of ideas and a limited schedule, I began to put those floating stories that I had conjured up—the same ones that had been swirling around in my head for decades—down on paper.

Like the floodgates had opened, the words streamed out of my mind, through my fingers, onto the keyboard and what I stared at directly in front of me after a few months of writing was a finished product. Pages upon pages of the story as I knew it sprinkled with some of my creativity as it had been and as I had intended.

Except with one small difference. Now you could see it too.

I had written my first book. There it was, my humor and sarcasm jumping out on the pages while at the same time telling the world about my overly enthusiastic, bouncy golden retriever, Buddy. I had the title picked out. Finally Home.

Now, what was I to do with it? I knew nothing about publishing. Even less about marketing.

I did the research, and there it was in black and white. "Find an agent who will then find a publisher. You may get rejected over 5000 times before you find an agent."

5000 times?

I wasn't keen on that option. Then, like a green light, I moved forward to my next option.

With the advent of the Internet, I was shown an opportunity, presented in front of me. Another unexplored territory. Something I knew nothing about— Self-publishing. I'd never heard of it.

The word "indie" was something I had to research. But there it was.

So, I did it. I had written my book. I formatted it, uploaded it, created a cover and clicked the publish button.

Now, what?

I didn't expect anything, but I told a few people.

I waited a few days. I saw a few sales. Must be my friends, but the sales were on Kindle. None of my friends had a Kindle at the time. I feel as if I'm dating myself when I say no one had the Kindle. It was only a few years ago. How times have changed!

I asked around. No one I knew had purchased it. My book had gone mainstream. Strangers were buying it. Buddy's hilarious shenanigans were available for the world to see. His whimsical behavior was bringing smiles to people he had never even met. I then received fan mail. It was exhilarating. I'm still friends with many of those fans today!

I wanted to write more. I had plenty of ideas, after all! Where did I go from there?

I had dog stories I wanted to tell. Plenty of them. But...what about the other side of my brain? What other side? Ah, yes, there is a dark side. Isn't there always?

I grew up watching every Friday the 13th and the Omen series. I am keen on scary movies. I'm the type of person who wakes from a nightmare, becomes somewhat terror-stricken, and then writes it down in amazement of how truly bizarre it was.

Do I dare? Is it okay? Should I write a different genre? If you're a writer have you ever asked yourself that same question?

Whew. Deep breath. How do I go from writing about the safety and rescue of dogs to a psychological thriller? What will my readers think?

I had to take the chance. It's been done before, right?

I couldn't avoid writing it. The words haunted me like a recurring dream every evening. The chapters were forming by themselves screaming to get out and jump onto the nice, white, clean, blank Word document. My conversations with people were interrupted by the incessant need to write more ideas down. So I did. Strangely enough, I only had a "dumb phone" so my notes were still all written on sticky notes. Tons of them. All scattered around my purse.

My dreams needed to cultivate a story. And then the story needed to come out. And so it did. Three short months later, Unwanted Dreams was born. My first Thriller. Fiction, of course.

Non-fiction was easy to write in comparison. There was no question about where the story would go or which direction it would take. It was written easily because it had already happened.

Fiction was an entirely different animal.

I had written part of this paragraph in "Occupational Hazard" but it is so true. With writing, "I had to formulate an entire character list. In an hour, I had to change my mindset from a teenage boy to a young mother. I had to fall in love, seal off a crime scene, console a widow and hunt down a victim. I had to think like a killer. I had to feel powerful and then I had to be rendered helpless..."

When writing fiction of any kind, you don't just think like a writer, you become an actor. In your mind, your voice changes to become that of your character. Your diction changes. Your accent changes. You see seasons that have long past or a dark, dismal road for which you had never traveled. Thankfully.

It's an extraordinary revelation as you become one with your characters, and you learn to love them or even more bizarre, hate them.

It's a strange emotion that fulfills you when you can instill fear into not only your readers but into YOURSELF as you're writing! Or when you've written something so emotional that you burst into tears.

But...it was fun. And still is fun. I have tons of book titles with accompanying stories that I need to write. There's just not enough time in the day. I've taken the plunge of writing two distinctly different genres: dog stories and thrillers.

The differences are plenty. Two completely diverse ways of thinking. Not only in writing but in creating the cover and especially compiling the book trailer.

Unwanted Dreams unleashed an entirely different writing style than my books for dog lovers. It continued with Phobia, Evil's Door, Faces of Deception and Occupational Hazard.

Composing thrillers prompts a curious reaction from friends and relatives as they have known me forever, yet they wonder where these dark ideas come from and how long they've been inhabiting my mind. A more fearful reaction occurs when I say most come of the ideas from my dreams!

But don't worry. I'm quite normal. I just possess an overactive imagination that dares to come out and play once in a while!

What Are You Expecting?

As readers, we may think to ourselves, "what are we looking for in a writer." But how often does one pose the opposite question to a writer. "What are we looking for in our readers?"

Writing is an interesting craft, whether it is for pleasure, for business or a bit of both. In a very big way, it mimics that of a diary as you are putting yourself out there for the world to analyze, scrutinize, comment, praise or condemn.

When writing blogs, I've noticed that it differs greatly from writing a novel. With blogs, you can circulate your writing around the same topic, or you can vary it as much as you see fit. If an article isn't a big hit with your audience, you can write another one within a day's time.

Your writing may change as your moods change. One day you can write about yoga, and the next, how to make candles. It enables you to be as broad-minded or as focused as you want.

When writing a book, the playing field changes. For each novel that you finish, it consists of taking one idea and bringing it to fruition.

In both instances, the seed for that idea needs to be planted, tended to, refined and polished, regardless what the topic is.

The benefit of writing a book is that while writing, there is the tendency to get lost in your own story. For many, (or most perhaps), they use an outline and know exactly where the story is going from the moment they put pen to paper, or I should say, fingers to the keys.

I have a general idea of how I would like it to progress. As I focus on character development, sometimes that idea changes.

I write in two distinctly different genres. One is all things dog. Dog adoption, dog observations and puppy mills. The other is fictional thrillers. More specifically, psychological thrillers.

What Do You Want Your Readers to See?

So what did I want my readers to get out of it?

The answer to that is not as easy as one word or one sentence for that matter.

In Unwanted Dreams, without giving away too much of the plot, the antagonist was a surprise to me much as it was to many of my readers. My characters seemingly developed personalities all on their own and went in a different direction than I had planned.

Who was I to step in and stop them?

So here is what I had hoped.

I wanted the reader to feel a similar emotion as I did when I had written the scene. As a writer, in my own stories, I had made myself laugh, cry, and even become scared when a killer entered a darkened room!

I've had people email me expressing a fondness for a certain title, and talk about their love or hatred of a certain character. I think many will agree that it is a direct compliment to an author. It means the reader connected on a certain level to your story.

One reader wrote to tell me that Unwanted Dreams was an emotional rollercoaster and that she never thought she'd feel the wide range of emotions that encompassed her as she read!

Until that point, I didn't realize it, but she was dead-on. While Unwanted Dreams is in fact, a thriller, you can't help but feel a sense of happiness, loathing, sadness, and anger all in one book. It's one of those stories that make you think afterward. And that was, indeed my goal.

I had hoped that whoever read that story would be ready for an interesting ride. One that captivated them, one that shifted gears, a story that threw them for a loop when they were expecting something else to happen. One that made them put down the book when they were finished and ask the question...could that story have happened in real life?

When I write my dog-related books, I hope for a different kind of feeling. With Finally Home, I wanted to share those comical stories with my readers to bring a smile to their faces.

In Final Journey, my goal was much different. I had hoped to help those that are mourning their pets to cope. I wanted to send a message across that we dog lovers understand their grief, and they are not alone. I received emails from my readers saying how glad they were to read Final Journey as it helped them through a difficult time. That was all that I needed. What a great feeling.

My intention with The Paw Prints in the Sand series was to bring awareness about puppy mills and animal rescue.

In each dog-related book, I hoped to share my real-life experiences or in my fictional dog books, experiences that are similar to real life. I hoped to educate, make people aware and make people smile.

I believe that every person has a story to tell, an experience to share or a lesson to teach. Not just writers, but everybody.

As writers, however, we have a responsibility to at least bring something to the table, some unknown fact, interesting tidbit or a lighthearted escape from an otherwise hectic day.

Regardless of what I do write, my hope is that I can provide entertainment on a small scale and assistance in areas in which I am familiar. I'll never claim to be an expert on any topic, but I'll eagerly share what I do know. Some of my stories might be serious, some silly or funny, but I hope to enlighten in some way.

If you are going to write a book, once it's written, I do suggest to get an editor or editing program. Then, copyright your book to safeguard your hard work.

Most of all, enjoy life and be passionate while you're writing it!

Epilogue:

Dogs have inspired me to live life with a passion. They are the constant thing that keep me going every day, even when I'm having one of those I-don't-feel-like-getting-out-of-bed days. You know the ones I'm talking about. The days when you are just too tired to get anything done. I look at my dogs (who wouldn't let me sleep in anyway) and realize that even if I'm not at my best, they are. They deserve to get attention and happiness every single day. Their lives, after all, are considerably shorter than ours so each day should be a good one for them.

Observing each dog that I've been fortunate to live with or even just encounter has shown me a different perspective on life. They live each day with no expectations, but just appreciate the here and now. They don't fret about yesterday or live with anxiety about the future. They are compassionate souls who know how to appreciate a single blade of grass, as they sniff each one on their walks. They don't need technology to see what other dogs are doing. They don't gauge another one's worth by how much money they have. They aren't judgmental but use their keen senses to determine who is good and who is bad. They trust their instincts, know how to work hard, play hard and understand the true meaning of relaxation.

I won't say it's easy to follow their lead, but they are a constant reminder of exactly how to live. Without saying one human word, they convey their message loud and clear.

Live. And do so passionately.

Other Books by Elizabeth Parker

Thrillers:

Unwanted Dreams

Phobia

Evil's Door

Faces of Deception

Occupational   Hazard-Perfect Lies

Dog Books:

Finally Home: Lessons on Life from a Free-Spirited Dog

Final Journey: Buddys' Book

My Dog Does That!

Paw Prints in the Sand

Paw Prints in the Sand: Mission Accomplished

Hearts of Gold

Bark Out Loud!

Fur-Baby's Keepsake Book

Other:

"Purr" Baby's Mementos Book